HISTORY

OF

THE BALDWIN LOCOMOTIVE WORKS

1831-1920

DIRECTORS

WILLIAM L. AUSTIN, Rosemont, Pa.

ALBA B. JOHNSON, Rosemont, Pa.

SAMUEL M. VAUCLAIN, Rosemont, Pa.

SAMUEL F. PRYOR, New York, N. Y.

WILLIAM E. COREY, New York, N. Y.

SYDNEY E. HUTCHINSON, Philadelphia, Pa.

SIDNEY F. TYLER, Philadelphia, Pa.

B. DAWSON COLEMAN, Lebanon, Pa.

HAROLD T. WHITE, New York, N. Y.

THOMAS G. ASHTON, Philadelphia, Pa.

ARTHUR W. SEWALL, Philadelphia, Pa.

ARTHUR E. NEWBOLD, Philadelphia, Pa.

OFFICERS

ARTHUR E. NEWBOLD.	Chairman of the Board
WILLIAM L. AUSTIN	Vice-Chairman of the Board
SAMUEL M. VAUCLAIN	President
JOHN P. SYKES.	Vice-President in Charge of Manufacture
WILLIAM DEKRAFFT	Vice-President in Charge of Finance, and Treasurer
GRAFTON GREENOUGH	Vice-President in Charge of Domestic Sales
F. DE ST. PHALLE	Vice-President in Charge of Foreign Sales
JAMES MCNAUGHTON.	Consulting Vice-President
ARTHUR L. CHURCH	Secretary and Assistant Treasurer
A. B. EHST	Comptroller

MAIN OFFICE AND WORKS, PHILADELPHIA PLANT

THE BALDWIN LOCOMOTIVE WORKS

1831

MATTHIAS W. BALDWIN

1839

BALDWIN, VAIL & HUFTY

M. W. BALDWIN*   GEORGE VAIL*   GEORGE W. HUFTY*

1841

BALDWIN & VAIL

M. W. BALDWIN*   GEORGE VAIL*

1842

BALDWIN & WHITNEY

M. W. BALDWIN*   ASA WHITNEY*

1846

M. W. BALDWIN

1854

M. W. BALDWIN & CO.

M. W. BALDWIN*   MATTHEW BAIRD*

1867

M. BAIRD & CO.

MATTHEW BAIRD*   GEORGE BURNHAM*   CHARLES T. PARRY*

1870

M. BAIRD & CO.

MATTHEW BAIRD*   GEORGE BURNHAM*   CHARLES T. PARRY*
EDWARD H. WILLIAMS*   WILLIAM P. HENSZEY*   EDWARD LONGSTRETH*

1873

BURNHAM, PARRY, WILLIAMS & CO.

GEORGE BURNHAM*   CHARLES T. PARRY*   EDWARD H. WILLIAMS*
WILLIAM P. HENSZEY*   EDWARD LONGSTRETH*   JOHN H. CONVERSE*

1886

BURNHAM, PARRY, WILLIAMS & CO.

GEORGE BURNHAM*   CHARLES T. PARRY*   EDWARD H. WILLIAMS*
WILLIAM P. HENSZEY*   JOHN H. CONVERSE*   WILLIAM C. STROUD*
WILLIAM H. MORROW*   WILLIAM L. AUSTIN

1891

BURNHAM, WILLIAMS & CO.

GEORGE BURNHAM*   EDWARD H. WILLIAMS*   WILLIAM P. HENSZEY*
JOHN H. CONVERSE*   WILLIAM C. STROUD*   WILLIAM L. AUSTIN

1896

BURNHAM, WILLIAMS & CO.

GEORGE BURNHAM*   EDWARD H. WILLIAMS*   WILLIAM P. HENSZEY*
JOHN H. CONVERSE*   WILLIAM L. AUSTIN   SAMUEL M. VAUCLAIN
ALBA B. JOHNSON   GEORGE BURNHAM, JR.

1901

BURNHAM, WILLIAMS & CO.

GEORGE BURNHAM*   WILLIAM P. HENSZEY*   JOHN H. CONVERSE*
WILLIAM L. AUSTIN   SAMUEL M. VAUCLAIN   ALBA B. JOHNSON
GEORGE BURNHAM, JR.

1907

BURNHAM, WILLIAMS & CO.

GEORGE BURNHAM*   WILLIAM P. HENSZEY*   JOHN H. CONVERSE*
WILLIAM L. AUSTIN   SAMUEL M. VAUCLAIN   ALBA B. JOHNSON

1909

Incorporated under the Laws of Pennsylvania as
BALDWIN LOCOMOTIVE WORKS

1911

Incorporated under the Laws of Pennsylvania as
THE BALDWIN LOCOMOTIVE WORKS

*NOW DECEASED

BIRD'S EYE VIEW OF THE EDDYSTONE PLANT

The Baldwin Locomotive Works

THESE Works occupy nineteen and three-tenths acres in the heart of Philadelphia and five hundred and ninety-six acres at Eddystone, on the Delaware River, twelve miles below the city. The offices and principal machine shops are situated in the rectangle bounded on the north by Spring Garden Street, on the east by Broad Street, on the south by the Philadelphia and Reading Railway Subway and on the west by Nineteenth Street. There are also shops located on the line of the Philadelphia and Reading Railway at Twenty-sixth to Twenty-ninth Streets.

The Works dates its origin from the inception of steam railroads in America. Called into existence by the early requirements of the railroad interests of the country, it has grown with their growth and kept pace with their progress. It has reflected in its career the successive stages of American railroad practice, and has itself contributed largely to the development of the locomotive as it exists today. A history of The Baldwin Locomotive Works, therefore, is in a great measure, a record of the progress of locomotive engineering in this country, and as such cannot fail to be of interest to those who are concerned in this important element of our material progress.

MATTHIAS W. BALDWIN, the founder of the establishment, learned the trade of a jeweler, and entered the service of Fletcher & Gardiner, Jewelers and Silversmiths, Philadelphia, in 1817. Two years later he opened a small shop, in the same line of business, on his own account. The demand for articles of this character falling off, however, he formed a partnership in 1825, with David Mason, a machinist, in the manufacture of bookbinders' tools and cylinders for calico printing. Their shop was in a small alley which runs north from Walnut Street, above Fourth. They afterward removed to Minor Street, below Sixth. The business was so successful that steam power became necessary in carrying on their manufactures, and an engine was bought for the purpose. This proving unsatisfactory, Mr. Baldwin decided to design and construct one which should be specially adapted to the requirements of his shop. One of these requirements was that it should occupy the least possible space, and this was met by the construction of an upright engine on a novel and ingenious plan. On a bed-plate about five feet square an upright cylinder was placed; the piston rod connected to a cross-bar having two legs, turned downward, and sliding in grooves on the sides of the cylinder, which thus formed the guides. To the sides of these legs, at their lower ends, was connected by pivots an inverted U-shaped frame, prolonged at the arch into a single rod, which took hold of the crank of a fly wheel carried by upright standards on the bed-plate. It will be seen that the length of the ordinary separate guide-bars was thus saved, and the whole engine was brought within the smallest possible compass. The design of the machine was not only unique, but its workmanship was so excellent, and its efficiency so great, as readily to procure for Mr. Baldwin orders for additional stationary engines. His attention was thus turned to steam engineering, and the way was prepared for his grappling with the problem of the locomotive when the time should arrive.

MR. BALDWIN'S FIRST ENGINE

This original stationary engine, constructed prior to 1830, is still in good order and carefully preserved at the Works. It has successively supplied the power in six different departments as they have been opened, from time to time, in the growth of the business.

The manufacture of stationary steam engines thus took a prominent place in the establishment, and Mr. Mason shortly afterward withdrew from the partnership.

In 1829-30 the use of steam as a motive power on railroads had begun to engage the attention of American engineers. A few locomotives had been imported from England, and one (which, however, was not successful) had been constructed at the West Point Foundry, in New York City. To gratify the public interest in the new motor, Mr. Franklin Peale, then proprietor of the Philadelphia Museum, applied to Mr. Baldwin to construct a miniature locomotive for exhibition in his establishment. With the aid only of the imperfect published descriptions and sketches of the locomotives which had taken part in the Rainhill competition in England, Mr. Baldwin undertook the work, and on the 25th of April, 1831, the miniature locomotive was put in motion on a circular track made of pine boards covered with hoop iron, in the rooms of the Museum. Two small cars, containing seats for four passengers, were attached to it, and the novel spectacle attracted crowds of admiring spectators. Both anthracite and pine-knot coal were used as fuel, and the exhaust steam was discharged into the chimney, thus utilizing it to increase the draught.

The success of the model was such that, in the same year, Mr. Baldwin received an order for a locomotive from the Philadelphia, Germantown and Norristown Railroad Company, whose short line of six miles to Germantown was operated by horse power. The Camden and Amboy Railroad Company had shortly before imported a locomotive from England, which was stored in a shed at Bordentown. It had not yet been put together; but Mr. Baldwin, in company with his friend Mr. Peale, visited the spot, inspected the detached parts, and made a few memoranda of some of its principal dimensions. Guided by these figures and his experience with the Peale model, Mr. Baldwin commenced the task. The difficulties to be overcome in filling the order can hardly be appreciated at this day. There were few mechanics competent to do any part of the work on a locomotive. Suitable tools were with difficulty obtainable. Cylinders were bored by a chisel fixed in a block of wood and turned by hand. Blacksmiths able to weld a bar of iron exceeding one and one-quarter inches in thickness were few, or not to be had. It was necessary for Mr. Baldwin to do much of the work with his own hands, to educate the workmen who assisted him, and to improvise tools for the various processes.

The work was prosecuted, nevertheless, under all these difficulties, and the locomotive was fully completed, christened "Old Ironsides," and tried on the road, November 23, 1832.

The circumstances of the trial are fully preserved, and are given, farther on, in the extracts from the journals of the day. Despite some imperfections, naturally occurring in a first effort, and which were afterward to a great extent remedied, the engine was, for that early day, a marked and gratifying success. It was put at once into service, as appears from the company's advertisement three days after the trial, and did duty on the Germantown road and others for over a score of years.

The "Ironsides" was a four-wheeled engine, modeled essentially on the English practice of that day, as shown in the "Planet" class, and weighed, in running order, something over five tons. The rear or driving wheels were fifty-four inches in

THE "OLD IRONSIDES," 1832

diameter on a crank axle placed in front of the firebox. The cranks were thirty-nine inches from center to center. The front wheels, which were simply carrying wheels, were forty-five inches in diameter, on an axle placed just back of the cylinders. The cylinders were nine and one-half inches in diameter by eighteen inches stroke, and were attached horizontally to the outside of the smokebox, which was D-shaped, with the sides receding inwardly, so as to bring the center line of each cylinder in line with the center of the crank. The wheels were made with heavy cast-iron hubs, wooden spokes and rims, and wrought-iron tires. The frame was of wood, placed outside the wheels. The boiler was thirty inches in diameter, and contained seventy-two copper flues, one and one-half inches in diameter and seven feet long. The tender was a four-wheeled platform, with wooden sides and back, carrying an iron box for a water tank, inclosed in a wooden casing, and with a space for fuel in front. The engine had no cab. The valve motion was at first given by a single loose eccentric for each cylinder, placed on the axle between the crank and the hub of the wheel. On the inside of the eccentric was a half-circular slot, running half way around. A stop was fastened to the axle at the arm of the crank, terminating in a pin which projected into the slot. The engine was reversed by changing the position of the eccentric on the axle by a lever operated from the footboard. This form of valve motion was, however, shortly afterward changed, and a single fixed eccentric for each cylinder substituted. The rock shafts, which were under the footboard, had arms above and below, and the eccentric straps had each a forked rod, with a hook, or an upper and lower latch or pin, at their extremities, to engage with the upper or lower arm of the rock shaft. The eccentric rods were raised or lowered by a double treadle, so as to connect with the upper or lower arm of the rock shaft, according as forward or backward gear was desired. A peculiarity in the exhaust of the "Ironsides" was that there was only a single straight pipe running across from one cylinder to the other, with an opening in the upper side of the pipe, midway between the cylinders, to which was attached at right angles the perpendicular pipe into the chimney. The cylinders, therefore, exhausted against each other; and it was found, after the engine had been put in use, that this was a serious objection. This defect was afterward remedied by turning each exhaust pipe upward into the chimney substantially as it is now done. The steam joints were made with canvas and red lead, as was the practice in English locomotives, and in consequence much trouble was caused, from time to time, by leaking.

The price of the engine was to have been $4000, but some difficulty was found in procuring a settlement. The company claimed that the engine did not perform according to contract; and objection was also made to some of the defects alluded to.

After these had been corrected as far as possible, however, Mr. Baldwin finally succeeded in effecting a compromise settlement, and received from the Company $3500 for the machine.

The results of the trial and the impression produced by it on the public mind may be gathered from the following extracts from the newspapers of the day:

The *United States Gazette*, of November 24, 1832, remarked:

"A most gratifying experiment was made yesterday afternoon on the Philadelphia, Germantown and Norristown Railroad. The beautiful locomotive engine and tender, built by Mr. Baldwin, of this city, whose reputation as an ingenious machinist is well known, were for the first time placed on the road. The engine traveled about six miles, working with perfect accuracy and ease in all its parts, and with great velocity."

The *Chronicle* of the same date noticed the trial more at length, as follows:

"It gives us pleasure to state that the locomotive engine built by our townsman, M. W. Baldwin, has proved highly successful. In the presence of several gentlemen of science and information on such subjects, the engine was yesterday placed upon the road for the first time. All her parts had been previously highly finished and fitted together in Mr. Baldwin's factory. She was taken apart on Tuesday, and removed to the Company's depot, and yesterday morning she was completely together, ready for travel. After the regular passenger cars had arrived from Germantown in the afternoon, the tracks being clear, preparation was made for her starting. The placing fire in the furnace and raising steam occupied twenty minutes. The engine (with her tender) moved from the depot in beautiful style, working with great ease and uniformity. She proceeded about half a mile beyond the Union Tavern, at the township line, and returned immediately, a distance of six miles, at a speed of about twenty-eight miles to the hour, her speed having been slackened at all the road crossings, and it being after dark, but a portion of her power was used. It is needless to say that the spectators were delighted. From this experiment there is every reason to believe this engine will draw thirty tons gross, at an average speed of forty miles an hour, on a level road. The principal superiority of the engine over any of the English ones known consists in the light weight—which is but between four and five tons—her small bulk, and the simplicity of her working machinery. We rejoice at the result of this experiment, as it conclusively shows that Philadelphia, always famous for the skill of her mechanics, is enabled to produce steam engines for railroads combining so many superior qualities as to warrant the belief that her mechanics will hereafter supply nearly all the public works of this description in the country."

On subsequent trials, the "Ironsides" attained a speed of thirty miles per hour, with its usual train attached. So great were the wonder and curiosity which attached to such a prodigy, that people flocked to see the marvel, and eagerly bought the privilege of riding after the strange monster. The officers of the road were not slow to avail themselves of the public interest to increase their passenger receipts, and the following advertisement from *Poulson's American Daily Advertiser*, of November 26, 1832, will show that as yet they regarded the new machine rather as a curiosity and a bait to allure travel than as a practical every-day servant.

This announcement did not mean that in wet weather horses *would be attached to the locomotive* to aid it in drawing the train, but that the usual horse cars would be employed in making the trips upon the road without the engine.

Upon making the first trip to Germantown with a passenger train with the "Ironsides," one of the drivers slipped upon the axle, causing the wheels to track less than the gauge of the road and drop in between the rails. It was also discovered that the valve arrangement of the pumps was defective, and they failed to supply the boiler with water. The shifting of the driving wheel upon the axle fastened the eccentric, so that it would not operate in backward motion. These mishaps caused delay, and prevented the engine from reaching its destination, to the great disappointment of all concerned. They were corrected in a few days, and the machine was used in experimenting upon its efficiency, making occasional trips with trains to Germantown. The road had an ascending grade, nearly uniform, of thirty-two feet per mile, and for the last half mile of forty-five feet per mile, and it was found that the engine was too light for the business of the road upon these grades.

Such was Mr. Baldwin's first locomotive; and it is related of him that his discouragement at the difficulties which he had undergone in building it, and in finally procuring a settlement for it, was such that he remarked to one of his friends, with much decision, "That is our last locomotive."

It was some time before he received an order for another, but meanwhile the subject had become singularly fascinating to him, and occupied his mind so fully that he was eager to work out his new ideas in a tangible form.

Shortly after the "Ironsides" had been placed on the Germantown road, Mr. E. L. Miller, of Charleston, S. C., came to Philadelphia and made a careful examination of the machine. Mr. Miller had, in 1830, contracted to furnish a locomotive to the Charleston and Hamburg Railroad Company, and accordingly the engine "Best Friend" had been built under his direction at the West Point Foundry, New York. After inspecting the "Ironsides," he suggested to Mr. Baldwin to visit the Mohawk and Hudson Railroad, and examine an English locomotive which had been placed on that road in July, 1831, by Messrs. Robert Stephenson & Co., of Newcastle, England. It was originally a four-wheeled engine of the "Planet" type, with horizontal cylinders and crank axle. The front wheels of this engine were removed about a year after the machine was put at work,

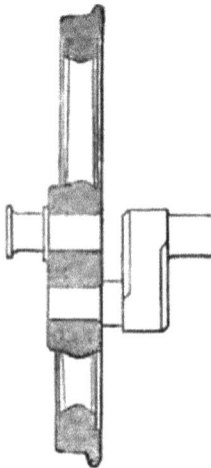

HALF-CRANK

and a four-wheeled swiveling or "bogie" truck substituted. The result of Mr. Baldwin's investigations was the adoption of this design, but with some important improvements. Among these was the "half-crank," which he devised on his return from this trip, and which he patented September 10, 1834. In this form of crank, the outer arm is omitted, and the wrist is fixed in a spoke of the wheel. In other words, the wheel itself formed one arm of the crank. The result sought and gained was that the cranks were strengthened, and, being at the extremities of the axle, the boiler could be made larger in diameter and placed lower. The driving axle could also be placed back of the firebox; the connecting rods passing by the sides of the firebox and taking hold inside of the wheels. This arrangement of the crank also involved the placing of the cylinders outside the smokebox, as was done on the "Ironsides."

By the time the order for the second locomotive was received, Mr. Baldwin had matured this device and was prepared to embody it in practical form. The order came from Mr. E. L. Miller, in behalf of the Charleston and Hamburg Railroad Company, and the engine bore his name, and was completed February 18, 1834. It was on six wheels; one pair being drivers, four and one-half feet in diameter, with half-crank axle placed back of the firebox as above described, and the four front wheels combined

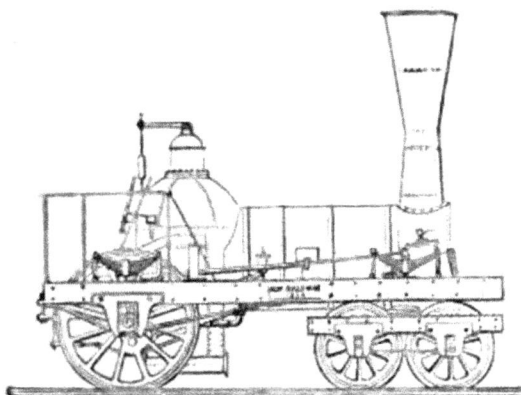

BALDWIN LOCOMOTIVE, 1834

in a swiveling truck. The driving wheels, it should be observed, were cast in solid bell metal. The combined wood and iron wheels used on the "Ironsides" had proved objectionable, and Mr. Baldwin, in his endeavors to find a satisfactory substitute, had recourse to brass. June 29, 1833, he took out a patent for a cast-brass wheel, his idea being that by varying the hardness of the metal the adhesion of the drivers on the rails could be increased or diminished at will. The brass wheels on the "Miller," however, soon wore out, and the experiment with this metal was not repeated. The "E. L. Miller" had cylinders ten inches in diameter; stroke of piston, sixteen inches; and weighed, with water in the boiler, seven tons eight hundred-weight. The boiler had a high dome over the firebox; and this form of construction, it may be noted, was followed, with a few exceptions, for many years.

The valve motion was given by a single fixed eccentric for each cylinder. Each eccentric strap had two arms attached to it, one above and the other below, and, as the driving axle was back of the firebox, these arms were prolonged backward under the footboard, with a hook on the inner side of the end of each. The rock shaft had arms above and below its axis, and the hooks of the two rods of each eccentric were moved by hand levers so as to engage with either arm, thus producing backward or forward gear. This form of single eccentric, peculiar to Mr. Baldwin, was in the interest of simplicity in the working parts, and was adhered to for some years. It gave rise to an animated controversy among mechanics as to whether, with its use, it was possible to get a lead on the valve in both directions. Many maintained that this was impracticable; but Mr. Baldwin demonstrated by actual experience that the reverse was the case.

Meanwhile the Commonwealth of Pennsylvania had given Mr. Baldwin an order for a locomotive for the State Road, as it was then called, from Philadelphia to Columbia, which, up to that time, had been worked by horses. This engine, called the "Lancaster," was completed in June, 1834. It was similar to the "Miller," and weighed seventeen thousand pounds. After it was placed in service, the records show that it hauled at one time nineteen loaded burden cars over the highest grades between Philadelphia and Columbia. This was characterized at that time by the officers of the road as an "unprecedented performance." The success of the machine on its trial trips was such that the Legislature decided to adopt steam power for working the road, and Mr. Baldwin received orders for several additional locomotives. Two others were accordingly delivered to the State in September and November respectively of that year, and one was also built and delivered to the Philadelphia and Trenton Railroad

Company during the same season. This latter engine, which was put in service October 21, 1834, averaged twenty-one thousand miles per year to September 15, 1840.

Five locomotives were thus completed in 1834, and the new business was fairly under way. The building in Lodge Alley, to which Mr. Baldwin had removed from Minor Street, and where

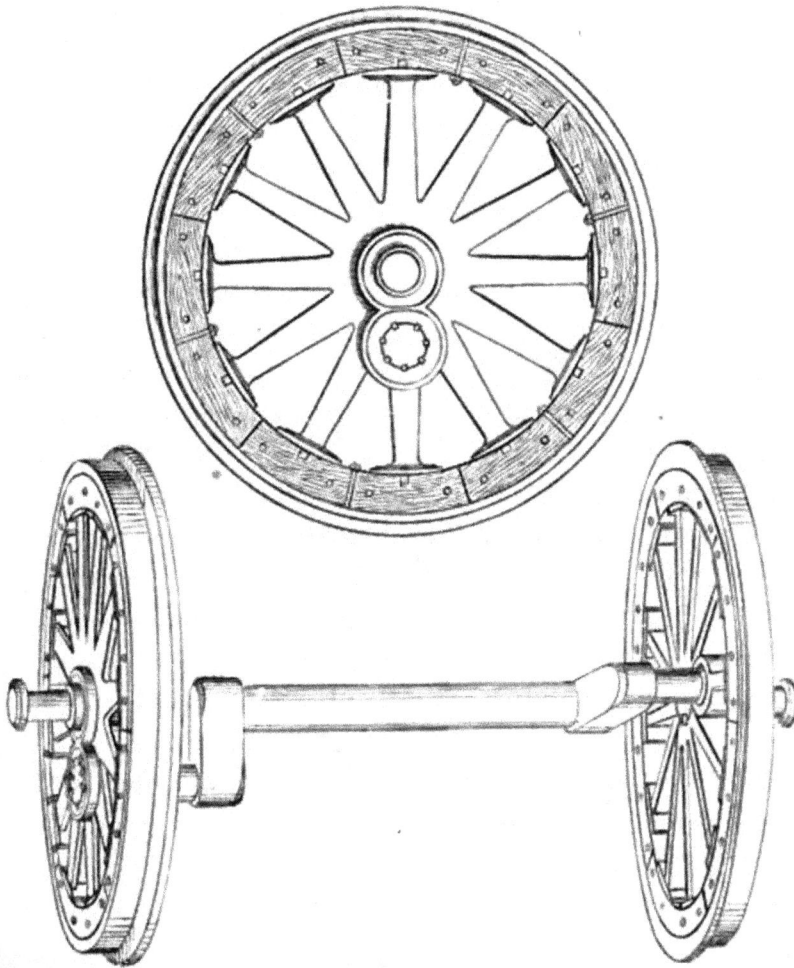

BALDWIN COMPOUND WOOD AND IRON WHEELS, 1834

these engines were constructed, began to be found too contracted, and another removal was decided upon. A location on Broad and Hamilton Streets (the site, in part, of the present works) was selected, and a three-story L-shaped brick building, fronting on both streets, erected. This was completed and the business removed to it during the following year (1835). Mr. Baldwin's stationary engine, described on page 8, was placed in service in the new shop by Mr. Andrew C. Vauclain, father of Mr. Samuel M. Vauclain, who is now President of the Company. The original building was partially destroyed by fire in 1884, and was replaced by a four-story brick structure.

These early locomotives, built in 1834, were the types of Mr. Baldwin's practice for some years. All, or nearly all of them, embraced several important devices, which were the results of his study and experiments up to that time. The devices referred to were patented September 10, 1834, and the same patent covered the following four inventions, *viz.*:

1.   The half-crank, and method of attaching it to the driving wheel. (This has already been described.)

2.   A new mode of constructing the wheels of locomotive engines and cars. In this the hub and spokes were of cast iron, cast together. The spokes were cast without a rim, and terminated in segment flanges, each spoke having a separate flange disconnected from its neighbors. By this means, it was claimed, the injurious effect of the unequal expansion of the materials composing the wheels was lessened or altogether prevented. The flanges bore against wooden felloes, made in two thicknesses, and put together so as to break joints. Tenons or pins projected from the flanges into openings made in the wooden felloes, to keep them in place. Around the whole the tire was passed and secured by bolts. The sketch on page 17 shows the device.

3.   A new mode of forming the joints of steam and other tubes. This was Mr. Baldwin's invention of ground joints for steam pipes, which was a very valuable improvement over previous methods of making joints with red-lead packing, and which rendered it possible to carry a much higher pressure of steam.

4.   A new mode of forming the joints and other parts of the supply pump, and of locating the pump itself. This invention consisted in making the single guide bar hollow and using it for the pump barrel. The pump plunger was attached to the piston rod at a socket or sleeve formed for the purpose, and the hollow guide bar terminated in the vertical pump chamber. This chamber was made in two pieces, joined about midway between the induction and eduction pipes. This joint was ground steam-

tight, as were also the joints of the induction pipe with the bottom of the lower chamber, and the flange of the eduction pipe with the top of the upper chamber. All these parts were held together by a stirrup with a set-screw in its arched top, and the arrangement was such that by simply unscrewing this set-screw the different sections of the chamber, with all the valves, could be taken apart for cleaning or adjusting. The cut below illustrates the device.

It is probable that the five engines built during 1834 embodied all, or nearly all, these devices. They all had the half-

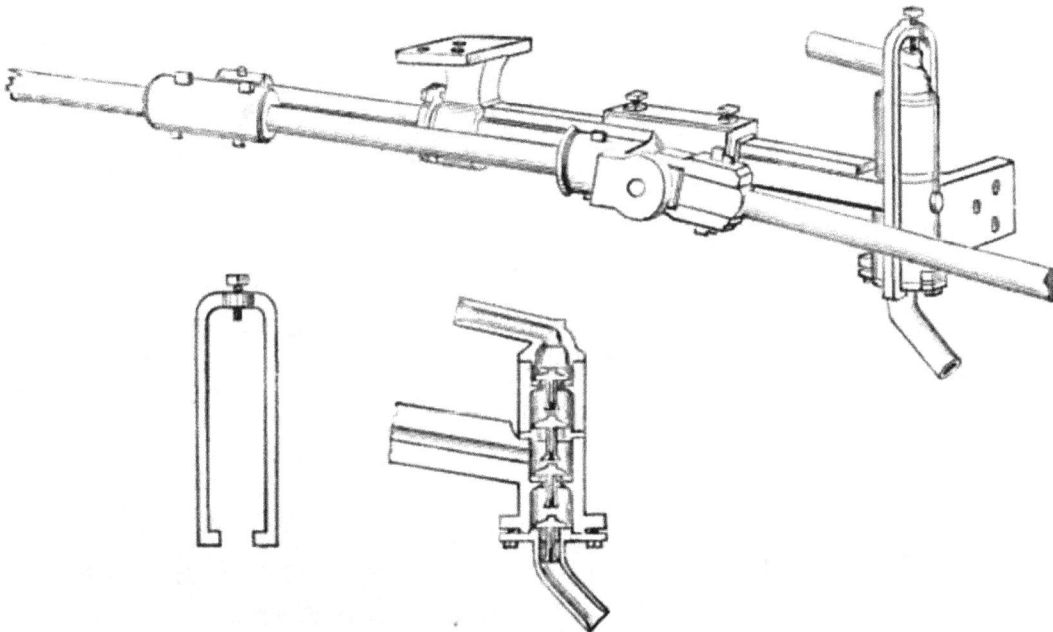

PUMP AND STIRRUP

crank, the ground joints for steam pipes (which were first made by Mr. Baldwin in 1833), and the pump formed in the guide bar, and all had the four-wheeled truck in front, and a single pair of drivers back of the firebox. On this position of the driving wheels Mr. Baldwin laid great stress, as it made a more even distribution of the weight, throwing about one-half on the drivers and one-half on the four-wheeled truck. It also extended the wheel base, making the engine much steadier and less damaging to the track. Mr. William Norris, who had established a locomotive works in Philadelphia in 1832, was at this time building a six-wheeled engine with a truck in front and the driving wheels placed in front of the firebox. Considerable rivalry naturally existed between the two manufacturers as to the comparative merits of their respective plans. In Mr. Norris' engine, the position of the driving axle in front of the firebox threw on it more of the weight of the engine, and thus increased the adhesion and the tractive power. Mr. Baldwin, however, maintained the superiority of his plan, as giving a better distribution of the weight and a longer wheel base, and consequently rendering the machine less destructive to the track. As the iron rails then in use were generally light, and much of the track was of wood, this feature was of some importance.

To the use of the ground joint for steam pipes, however, much of the success of his early engines was due. The English builders were making locomotives with canvas and red-lead joints, permitting a steam pressure of only sixty pounds per square inch to be carried, while Mr. Baldwin's machines were worked at one hundred and twenty pounds with ease. Several locomotives imported from England at about this period by the Commonwealth of Pennsylvania for the State Road (three of which were made by Stephenson) had canvas and red-lead joints, and their efficiency was so much less than that of the Baldwin engines, on account of this and other features of construction, that they were soon laid aside or sold.

In June, 1834, a patent was issued to Mr. E. L. Miller, by whom Mr. Baldwin's second engine was ordered, for a method of increasing the adhesion of a locomotive by throwing a part of the weight of the tender on the rear of the engine, thus increasing the weight on the drivers. Mr. Baldwin adopted this device on an engine built for the Philadelphia and Trenton Railroad Company, May, 1835, and thereafter used it largely, paying one hundred dollars royalty for each engine. Eventually (May 6, 1839) he bought the patent for nine thousand dollars, evidently considering that the device was especially valuable, if not indispensable, in order to render his engine as powerful, when required, as other patterns having the driving wheels in front of the firebox, and therefore utilizing more of the weight of the engine for adhesion.

In making the truck and tender wheels of these early locomotives, the hubs were cast in three pieces and afterward banded with wrought iron, the interstices being filled with spelter. This method of construction was adopted on account of the difficulty then found in casting a chilled wheel in one solid piece.

Early in 1835, the new shop on Broad Street was completed and occupied. Mr. Baldwin's attention was thenceforward given to locomotive building exclusively, except that a stationary engine was occasionally constructed.

In May, 1835, his eleventh locomotive, the "Black Hawk," was delivered to the Philadelphia and Trenton Railroad Company. This was the first outside-connected engine of his build. It was also the first engine on which the Miller device of attaching part of the weight of the tender to the engine was employed. On the eighteenth engine, the "Brandywine," built for the Philadelphia and Columbia Railroad Company, brass tires were used on the driving wheels, for the purpose of obtaining more adhesion; but they wore out rapidly and were replaced with iron.

April 3, 1835, Mr. Baldwin took out a patent for certain improvements in the wheels and tubes of locomotive engines. That relating to the wheels provided for casting the hub and spokes together, and having the spokes terminate in segments of a rim, as described in his patent of September 10, 1834. Between the ends of the spokes and the tires, wood was interposed, and the tire might be either of wrought iron or of chilled cast iron. The intention was expressed of making the tire usually of cast iron chilled. The main object, however, was declared to be the interposition between the spokes and the rim of a layer of wood or other substance possessing some degree of elasticity. This method of making driving wheels was followed for several years, the tires being made with a shoulder. See illustration on page 22.

The improvement in locomotive tubes consisted in driving a copper ferrule or thimble on the outside of the end of the tube, and soldering it in place, instead of driving a ferrule into the tube as had previously been the practice. The object of the latter method had been to make a tight joint with the tube sheet; but by putting the ferrule on the outside of the tube, not only was the joint made as tight as before, but the tube was strengthened, and left unobstructed throughout to the full extent of its diameter. This method of setting flues has been generally followed in the Works from that date to the present, the only difference being that, at this time, with iron or steel tubes, the end is swedged down, the copper ferrule brazed on, and the end of the tube turned or riveted over against the copper thimble and the flue sheet to make the joint perfect.

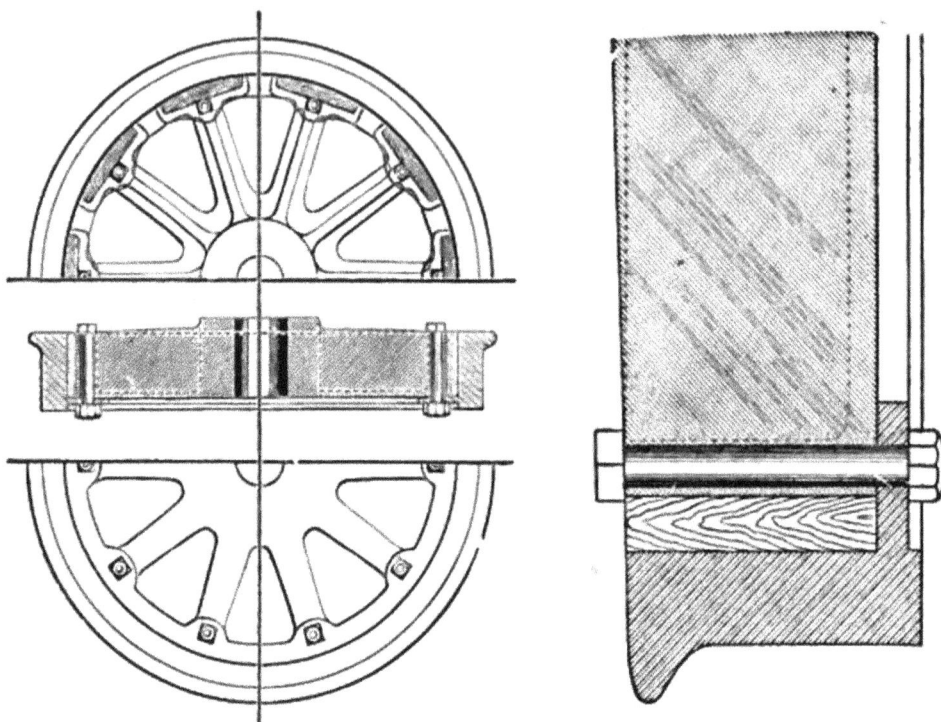

DRIVING WHEELS, PATENTED SEPTEMBER, 1834

Fourteen engines were constructed in 1835; forty in 1836; forty in 1837; twenty-three in 1838; twenty-six in 1839, and nine in 1840. During all these years the general design continued the same; but, in compliance with the demand for more power, three sizes were furnished, as follows:

First class— Cylinders, 12½ × 16; weight loaded, 26,000 pounds.
Second class—   "   12 × 16;   "   "   23,000   "
Third class—   "   10½ × 16;   "   "   20,000   "

Mr. Baldwin fully believed, in 1838, that the first class engine was as heavy as would be called for, and he declared that it was as large as he intended to make. Most of the engines were built with the half-crank, but occasionally an outside-connected machine was turned out. These latter, however, failed to give as complete satisfaction as the half-crank machine. The drivers were generally four and one-half feet in diameter.

A patent was issued to Mr. Baldwin, August 17, 1835, for his device of cylindrical pedestals. In this method of construction, the pedestal was of cast iron, and was bored in a lathe so as to form two concave jaws. The boxes were also turned in a lathe so that their vertical ends were cylindrical, and they were thus fitted in the pedestals. This method of fitting up pedestals and boxes was cheap and effective, and was used for some years for the driving and tender wheels.

As showing the estimation in which these early engines were held, it may not be out of place to refer to the opinions of some of the railroad managers of that period.

Mr. L. A. Sykes, engineer of the New Jersey Transportation Company, under date of June 12, 1838, wrote that he could draw with his engines twenty four-wheeled cars with twenty-six passengers each, at a speed of twenty to twenty-five miles per hour, over grades of twenty-six feet per mile. "As to simplicity of construction," he adds, "small liability to get out of order, economy of repairs, and ease to the road, I fully believe Mr. Baldwin's engines stand unrivalled. I consider the simplicity of the engine, the arrangement of the working parts, and the distribution of the weight, far superior to any engine I have ever seen, either of American or English manufacture, and I have not the least hesitation in saying that Mr. Baldwin's engine will do the same amount of work with much less repairs, either to the engine or the track, than any other engine in use."

L. G. Cannon, President of the Rensselaer and Saratoga Railroad Company, writes: "Your engines will, in performance and cost of repairs, bear comparison with any other engine made in this or any other country."

Some of Mr. Baldwin's engines on the State Road, in 1837, cost, for repairs, only from one and two-tenths to one and six-tenths cents per mile. It is noted that the engine "West Chester," on the same road, weighing twenty thousand seven hundred and thirty-five pounds (ten thousand four hundred and seventy-five on drivers), drew fifty-one cars (four-wheeled), weighing two hundred and eighty-nine net tons, over the road, some of the track being of wood covered with strap-rail.

The financial difficulties of 1836 and 1837, which brought ruin upon so many, did not leave Mr. Baldwin unscathed. His embarrassments became so great that he was unable to proceed, and was forced to call his creditors together for a settlement. After offering to surrender all his property, his shop, tools, house and everything, if they so desired—all of which would realize only about twenty-five per cent. of their claims—he proposed to them that they should permit him to go on with the business, and in three years he would pay the full amount of all claims, principal and interest. This was finally acceded to, and the promise was in effect fulfilled, although not without an extension of two years beyond the time originally proposed.

In May, 1837, the number of hands employed was three hundred, but this number was reduced weekly, owing to the falling off in the demand for engines.

These financial troubles had their effect on the demand for locomotives, as will be seen in the decrease in the number built in 1838, 1839 and 1840; and this result was furthered by the establishment of several other locomotive works, and the introduction of other patterns of engines.

The changes and improvements in details made during these years may be summed up as follows:

The subject of burning anthracite coal had engaged much attention. In October, 1836, Mr. Baldwin secured a patent for a grate or fireplace which could be detached from the engine at pleasure, and a new one with a fresh coal fire substituted. The intention was to have the grate with freshly ignited coal all ready for the engine on its arrival at a station, and placed between the rails over suitable levers, by which it could be attached quickly to the firebox. It is needless to say that this was never practiced. In January, 1838, however, Mr. Baldwin was experimenting with the consumption of coal on the Germantown road, and in July of the same year the records show that he was making a locomotive to burn coal, part of the arrangement being to blow the fire with a fan.

The first locomotives for export were built during this year. They were shipped to Cuba, to the order of Alfred Cruger, and bore the builder's numbers 104 and 105. These locomotives were completed in the spring and summer, and were followed by a third later in the year.

Up to 1838, Mr. Baldwin had made both driving and truck wheels with wrought tires, but during that year chilled wheels for engine and tender trucks were adopted. His tires were furnished by Messrs. S. Vail & Son, Morristown, N. J., who made the only tires then obtainable in America. They were very thin, being only one inch to one and one-half inches thick; and Mr. Baldwin, in importing some tires from England at that time, insisted on their being made double the ordinary thickness. The manufacturers at first objected and ridiculed the idea, the practice being to use two tires when extra thickness was wanted, but finally they consented to meet his requirements.

All his engines thus far had the single eccentric for each valve, but at about this period double eccentrics were adopted, each terminating in a straight hook, and reversed by hand levers.

At this early period, Mr. Baldwin had begun to feel the necessity of making all like parts of locomotives of the same class in such manner as to be absolutely interchangeable. Steps were taken in this direction, but it was not until many years afterward that the system of standard gauges was perfected, which soon became a distinguishing feature in the establishment.

In March, 1839, Mr. Baldwin's records show that he was building a number of outside-connected engines, and had succeeded in making them strong and durable. He was also making a new chilled wheel, and one which he thought would not break.

On the one hundred and thirty-sixth locomotive, completed October 18, 1839, for the Philadelphia, Germantown and Norristown Railroad, the old pattern of wooden frame was abandoned, and no outside frame whatever was employed—the machinery, as well as the truck and the pedestals of the driving axles, being attached directly to the naked boiler. The wooden frame thenceforward disappeared gradually, and an iron frame took its place. Another innovation was the adoption of eight-wheeled tenders, the first of which was built at about this period.

On April 8, 1839, Mr. Baldwin associated with himself Messrs. Vail & Hufty, and the business was conducted under the firm name of Baldwin, Vail & Hufty until 1841, when Mr. Hufty withdrew, and Baldwin & Vail continued the copartnership until 1842.

The time had now arrived when the increase of business on railroads demanded more powerful locomotives. It had for some years been felt that for freight traffic the engine with one pair of drivers was insufficient. Mr. Baldwin's engine had the single pair of drivers placed back of the firebox; that made by Mr. Norris, one pair in front of the firebox. An engine with two pairs of drivers, one pair in front and one pair behind the firebox, was the next logical step, and Mr. Henry R. Campbell, of Philadelphia, was the first to carry this design into execution. Mr. Campbell was the Chief Engineer of the Germantown Railroad when the "Ironsides" was placed on that line, and had since given much attention to the subject of locomotive construction. February 5, 1836, Mr. Campbell secured a patent for an eight-wheeled engine with four drivers connected, and a four-wheeled truck in front; and subsequently contracted with James Brooks, of Philadelphia, to build for him such a machine. The work was begun March 16, 1836, and the engine was completed May 8, 1837. This was the first eight-wheeled engine of this design, and from it the American type locomotive of today takes its origin. The engine lacked, however, one essential feature; there were no equalizing beams between the drivers, and nothing but the ordinary steel springs over each journal of the driving axles to equalize the weight upon them. It remained for Messrs. Eastwick & Harrison to supply this deficiency; and in 1837 that firm constructed at their shop in Philadelphia, a locomotive on this plan, but with the driving axles running in a separate square frame, connected to the main frame above it by a single central bearing on each side. This engine had cylinders twelve by eighteen, four coupled driving wheels, forty-four inches in diameter, carrying eight of the twelve tons constituting the total weight. Subsequently, Mr. Joseph Harrison, Jr., of the same firm, substituted "equalizing beams" on engines of this plan afterward constructed by them, substantially in the same manner as since generally employed.

In the *American Railroad Journal* of July 30, 1836, a wood-cut showing Mr. Campbell's engine, together with an elaborate calculation of the effective power of an engine on this plan, by William J. Lewis, Esq., Civil Engineer, was published, with a table showing its performance upon grades ranging from a dead level to a rise of one hundred feet per mile. Mr. Campbell stated that his experience at that time (1835-36) convinced him that grades of one hundred feet rise per mile would, if roads were judiciously located, carry railroads over any of the mountain passes in America, without the use of planes with stationary steam power, or, as a general rule, of costly tunnels—an opinion very extensively verified by the experience of the country since that date.

A step had thus been taken toward a plan of locomotive having more adhesive power. Mr. Baldwin, however, was slow to adopt the new design. He naturally regarded innovations with distrust. He had done much to perfect the old pattern of engine, and had built over a hundred of them, which were in successful operation on various railroads. Many of the details were the subjects of his several patents, and had been greatly simplified in his practice. In fact, simplicity in all the working parts had been so largely his aim, that it was natural that he should distrust any plan involving additional machinery, and he regarded the new design as only an experiment at best. In November, 1838, he wrote to a correspondent that he did not think there was any advantage in the eight-wheeled engine. There being three points in contact, it could not turn a curve, he argued, without slipping one or the other pair of wheels sideways. Another objection was in the multiplicity of machinery and the difficulty in maintaining four driving wheels all of exactly the same size. Some means, however, of getting more adhesion must be had, and the result of his reflections upon this subject was the project of a "geared engine." In August, 1839, he took steps to secure a patent for such a machine, and December 31, 1840, letters patent were granted him for the device. In this engine an independent shaft or axle was placed between the two axles of the truck, and connected by cranks and coupling rods with cranks on the outside of the driving wheels. This shaft had a central cog-wheel engaging on each side with intermediate cog-wheels, which in turn geared into cog-wheels on each truck axle. The intermediate cog-wheels had wide teeth, so that the truck could pivot while the main shaft remained parallel with the driving axle. The diameters of the cog-wheels were, of course, in such proportion to the driving and truck wheels that the latter should revolve as much oftener than the drivers as their smaller size might require. Of the success of this machine for freight service, Mr. Baldwin was very sanguine. One was put in hand at once, completed in August, 1841, and eventually sold to the Sugarloaf Coal Company. It was an inside-connected engine, weighing thirty thousand pounds, of which eleven thousand seven hundred and seventy-five pounds were on the drivers, and eighteen thousand three hundred and thirty-five on the truck. The driving wheels were forty-four and the truck wheels thirty-three inches in diameter. The cylinders were thirteen inches in diameter by sixteen inches stroke. On a trial of the engine upon the Philadelphia and Reading Railroad, it hauled five hundred and ninety tons from Reading to Philadelphia—a distance of fifty-four miles—in five hours and twenty-two minutes. The superintendent of the road, in writing of the trial, remarked that this train was unprecedented in length and weight both in America and Europe. The performance was noticed in favorable terms by the Philadelphia newspapers, and was made the subject of a report by the Committee on Science and Arts of the Franklin Institute, who strongly recommended this plan of engine for freight service. The success of the trial led Mr. Baldwin at first to believe that the geared engine would be generally adopted for freight traffic; but in this he was disappointed. No further demand was made for such machines, and no more of them were built.

In 1840, Mr. Baldwin received an order, through August Belmont, Esq., of New York, for a locomotive for Austria, and had nearly completed one which was calculated to do the work required, when he learned that only sixty pounds pressure of steam was admissible, whereas his engine was designed to use steam at one hundred pounds and over. He accordingly constructed another, meeting this requirement, and shipped it in the following year. This engine, it may be noted, had a kind of link motion, agreeably to the specification received, and was the first of his make upon which the link was introduced.

Mr. Baldwin's patent of December 31, 1840, already referred to as covering his geared engine, embraced several other devices, as follows:

1. A method of operating a fan, or blowing wheel, for the purpose of blowing the fire. The fan was to be placed under the footboard, and driven by the friction of a grooved pulley in contact with the flange of the driving wheel.

2. The substitution of a metallic stuffing consisting of wire, for the hemp, wool, or other material which had been employed in stuffing boxes.

3. The placing of the springs of the engine truck so as to obviate the evil of the locking of the wheels when the truck frame vibrates from the center pin vertically. Spiral as well as semi-elliptic springs, placed at each end of the truck frame, were specified. The spiral spring is described as received in two cups, one above and one below. The cups were connected together at their centers, by a pin upon one and a socket in the other, so that the cups could approach toward or recede from each other and still preserve their parallelism.

4. An improvement in the manner of constructing the iron frames of locomotives, by making the pedestals in one piece with, and constituting part of, the frames.

5. The employment of spiral springs in connection with cylindrical pedestals and boxes. A single spiral was at first used, but, not proving sufficiently strong, a combination or nest of spirals curving alternately in opposite directions was afterward employed. Each spiral had its bearing in a spiral recess in the pedestal.

In the specification of this patent a change in the method of making cylindrical pedestals and boxes is noted. Instead of boring and turning them in a lathe, they were cast to the required shape in chills. This method of construction was used for a time, but eventually a return was made to the original plan, as giving a more accurate job.

In 1842, Mr. Baldwin constructed, under an arrangement

with Mr. Ross Winans, three locomotives for the Western Railroad of Massachusetts, on a plan which had been designed by
that gentleman for freight traffic. These machines had upright

BALDWIN SIX-WHEELS-CONNECTED ENGINE, 1842

boilers and horizontal cylinders, which worked cranks on a shaft
bearing cog-wheels engaging with other cog-wheels on an intermediate shaft. This latter shaft had cranks coupled to four
driving wheels on each side. These engines were constructed
to burn anthracite coal. Their peculiarly uncouth appearance
earned for them the name of "crabs," and they were but short-
lived in service.

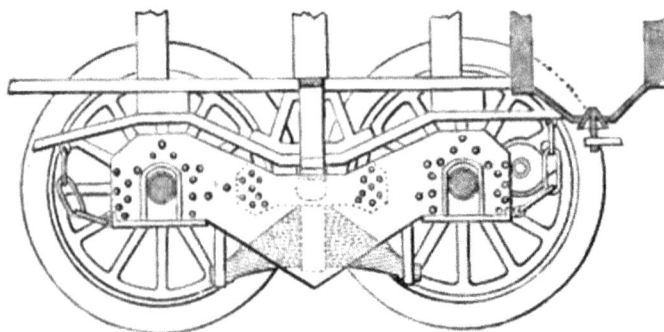

BALDWIN FLEXIBLE BEAM TRUCK, 1842—ELEVATION

But to return to the progress of Mr. Baldwin's locomotive
practice. Only eight engines were built in 1841. The geared
engine had not proved a success. It was unsatisfactory, as well
to its designer as to the railroad community. The problem of
utilizing more or all of the weight of the engine for adhesion

remained, in Mr. Baldwin's view, yet to be solved. The plan of coupling four or six wheels had long before been adopted in England, but on the short curves prevalent on American railroads he felt that something more was necessary. The wheels must not only be coupled, but at the same time must be free to adapt themselves to a curve. These two conditions were apparently incompatible, and to reconcile these inconsistencies was the task which Mr. Baldwin set himself to accomplish. He undertook it, too, at a time when his business had fallen off greatly and he was involved in the most serious financial embarrassments. The problem was constantly before him, and at length, during a sleepless night, its solution flashed across his mind. The plan so long sought for, and which, subsequently more than any other of his improvements or inventions, contributed to the foundation of his fortune, was his well-known six-wheels-connected locomo-

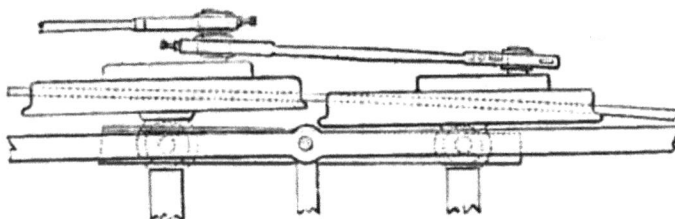

BALDWIN FLEXIBLE BEAM TRUCK, 1842—HALF PLAN

tive with the four front drivers combined in a flexible truck. For this machine Mr. Baldwin secured a patent, August 25, 1842. Its principal characteristic features are now matters of history, but they deserve here a brief mention. The engine was on six wheels, all connected as drivers. The rear wheels were placed rigidly in the frames, usually behind the firebox, with inside bearings. The cylinders were inclined, and with outside connections. The four remaining wheels had inside journals running in boxes held by two wide and deep wrought-iron beams, one on each side. These beams were unconnected, and entirely independent of each other. The pedestals formed in them were bored out cylindrically, and into them cylindrical boxes, as patented by him in 1835, were fitted. The engine frame on each side was directly over the beam, and a spherical pin, running down from the frame, bore in a socket in the beam midway between the two axles. It will thus be seen that each side beam independently could turn horizontally or vertically under the spherical pin, and the cylindrical boxes could also turn in the pedestals. Hence, in passing a curve, the middle pair of drivers could move laterally in one direction—say to the right—while the front pair could move in the opposite direction, or to the left; the two axles all the while remaining parallel to each other and to the rear driving axle. The operation of these beams was therefore like that of the parallel ruler. On a straight line the two beams and the two axles formed a rectangle; on curves, a parallelogram, the angles varying with the degree of curvature. The coupling rods were made with cylindrical brasses, thus forming ball-and-socket joints, to enable them to accommodate themselves to the lateral movements of the wheels. Colburn, in his "Locomotive Engineering," remarks of this arrangement of rods as follows:

"Geometrically, no doubt, this combination of wheels could only work properly around curves by a lengthening and shortening of the rods which served to couple the principal pair of driving wheels with the hind truck wheels. But if the coupling rods from the principal pair of driving wheels be five feet long, and if the beams of the truck frame be four feet long (the radius of curve described by the axle boxes around the spherical side bearings being two feet), then the total corresponding lengthening of the coupling rods, in order to allow the hind truck wheels to move one inch to one side, and the front wheels of the truck one inch to the other side of their normal position on a straight line would be $\sqrt{60^2+1^2}-60+24-\sqrt{24^2-1^2}$ 0.0275 inch, or less than one thirty-second of an inch. And if only one pair of driving wheels were thus coupled with a four-wheeled truck, the total wheel base being nine feet, the motion permitted by this slight elongation of the coupling rods (an elongation provided for by a trifling slackness in the brasses) would enable three pairs of wheels to stand without binding in a curve of only one hundred feet radius."

The first engine of the new plan was finished early in December, 1842, being one of fourteen engines constructed in that year, and was sent to the Georgia Railroad, on the order of Mr. J. Edgar Thomson, then Chief Engineer and Superintendent of that line. It weighed twelve tons, and drew, besides its own weight, two hundred and fifty tons up a grade of thirty-six feet to the mile.

Other orders soon followed. The new machine was received generally with great favor. The loads hauled by it exceeded anything so far known in American railroad practice, and sagacious managers hailed it as a means of largely reducing operating expenses. On the Central Railroad of Georgia, one of these twelve-ton engines drew nineteen eight-wheeled cars, with seven hundred and fifty bales of cotton, each bale weighing four hundred and fifty pounds, over maximum grades of thirty feet per mile, and the manager of the road declared that it could readily take one thousand bales. On the Philadelphia and Reading Railroad a similar engine of eighteen tons weight drew one hundred and fifty loaded cars (total weight of cars and lading, one thousand one hundred and thirty tons) from Schuylkill Haven to Philadelphia, at a speed of seven miles per hour. The regular load was one hundred loaded cars, which were hauled at a speed of from twelve to fifteen miles per hour on a level.

The following extract from a letter, dated August 10, 1844, of Mr. G. A. Nicolls, then superintendent of that line, gives the particulars of the performance of these machines, and shows the estimation in which they were held:

"We have had two of these engines in operation for about four weeks. Each engine weighs about forty thousand pounds with water and fuel, equally distributed on six wheels, all of which are coupled, thus gaining the whole adhesion of the engine's weight. Their cylinders are fifteen by eighteen inches.

"The daily allotted load of each of these engines is one hundred coal cars, each loaded with three and six-tenths tons of coal, and weighing two and fifteen one-hundredths tons each, empty; making a net weight of three hundred and sixty tons of coal carried, and a gross weight of train of five hundred and seventy-five tons, all of two thousand two hundred and forty pounds.

"This train is hauled over the ninety-four miles of the road, half of which is level, at the rate of twelve miles per hour; and with it the engine is able to make fourteen to fifteen miles per hour on a level.

"Were all the cars on the road of sufficient strength, and making the trip by daylight, nearly one-half being now performed at night, I have no doubt of these engines being quite equal to a load of eight hundred tons gross, as their average daily performance on any of the levels of our road, some of which are eight miles long.

"In strength of make, quality of workmanship, finish, and proportion of parts, I consider them equal to any, and superior to most, freight engines I have seen. They are remarkably easy on the rails, either in their vertical or horizontal action, from the equalization of their weight, and the improved truck under the forward part of the engine. This latter adapts itself to all the curves of the road, including some of seven hundred and sixteen feet radius in the main track, and moves with great ease around our turning Y curves at Richmond, of about three hundred feet radius.

"I consider these engines as near perfection, in the arrangement of their parts, and their general efficiency, as the present improvements in machinery and the locomotive engine will admit of. They are saving us thirty per cent. in every trip on the former cost of motive or engine power."

But the flexible beam truck also enabled Mr. Baldwin to meet the demand for an engine with four drivers connected. Other builders were making engines with four drivers and a four-wheeled truck, of the present American standard type. To compete with this design, Mr. Baldwin modified his six-wheels-connected engine by connecting only two of the three pairs of wheels as drivers, making the forward wheels of smaller diameter as leading wheels, but combining them with the front drivers in a flexible beam truck. The first engine on this plan was sent to the Erie and Kalamazoo Railroad, in October, 1843, and gave great satisfaction. The superintendent of the road was enthusiastic in its praise, and wrote to Mr. Baldwin that he doubted "if anything could be got up which would answer the business of the road so well." One was also sent to the Utica and Schenectady Railroad a few weeks later, of which the super-intendent remarked that "it worked beautifully, and there were not wagons enough to give it a full load." In this plan the leading wheels were usually made thirty-six and the drivers fifty-four inches in diameter.

This machine, of course, came in competition with the eight-wheeled engine having four drivers, and Mr. Baldwin claimed for his plan a decided superiority. In each case about two-thirds of the total weight was carried on the four drivers, and Mr. Baldwin maintained that his engine, having only six instead of eight wheels, was simpler and more effective.

At about this period Mr. Baldwin's attention was called by Mr. Levi Bissell to an "Air-spring" which the latter had devised, and which it was imagined was destined to be a cheap, effective, and perpetual spring. The device consisted of a small cylinder placed above the frame over the axle box, and having a piston fitted air-tight into it. The piston rod was to bear on the axle box and the proper quantity of air was to be pumped into the cylinder above the piston, and the cylinder then hermetically closed. The piston had a leather packing which was to be kept moist by some fluid (molasses was proposed) previously introduced into the cylinder. Mr. Baldwin at first proposed to equalize the weight between the two pairs of drivers by connecting two air springs on each side by a pipe, the use of an equalizing beam being covered by Messrs. Eastwick & Harrison's patent. The air springs were found, however, not to work practically, and were never applied. It may be added that a model of an equalizing air spring was exhibited by Mr. Joseph Harrison, Jr., at the Franklin Institute, in 1838 or 1839.

With the introduction of the new machine, business began at once to revive, and the tide of prosperity turned once more in Mr. Baldwin's favor. Twelve engines were constructed in 1843, all but four of them of the new pattern; twenty-two engines in 1844, all of the new pattern; and twenty-seven in 1845. Three of this number were of the old type, with one pair of drivers, but from that time forward the old pattern with the single pair of drivers disappeared from the practice of the establishment, save occasionally for exceptional purposes.

In 1842, the partnership with Mr. Vail was dissolved, and Mr. Asa Whitney, who had been superintendent of the Mohawk and Hudson Railroad, became a partner with Mr. Baldwin, and the firm continued as Baldwin & Whitney until 1846, when the latter withdrew to engage in the manufacture of car wheels, establishing the firm of A. Whitney & Sons, Philadelphia.

Mr. Whitney brought to the firm a railroad experience and thorough business talent. He introduced a system in many details of the management of the business, which Mr. Baldwin, whose mind was devoted more exclusively to mechanical subjects, had failed to establish or wholly ignored. The method at present in use in the establishment, of giving to each class of locomotives a distinctive designation, composed of a number and a letter, originated very shortly after Mr. Whitney's connection with the business. For the purpose of representing the different designs, sheets with engravings of locomotives were employed. The sheet showing the engine with one pair of drivers was marked B; that with two pairs, C; that with three, D; and that with four, E. Taking its rise from this circumstance, it became customary to designate as B engines those with one pair of drivers; as C engines, those with two pairs; as D engines, those with three pairs; and as E engines, those with four pairs. Shortly afterward, a number, indicating the weight in gross tons, was added. Thus the 12 D engine was one with three pairs of drivers and weighing twelve tons; the 12 C, an engine of same weight, but with only four wheels connected. A modification of this method of designating the several plans and sizes is still in use.

It will be observed that the classification as thus established began with the B engines. The letter A was reserved for an engine intended to run at very high speeds, and so designed that the driving wheels should make two revolutions for each reciprocation of the pistons. This was to be accomplished by means of gearing. The general plan of the engine was determined in Mr. Baldwin's mind, but was never carried into execution.

The adoption of the plan of six-wheels-connected engines opened the way at once to increasing their size. The weight being almost evenly distributed on six points, heavier machines were admissible, the weight on any one pair of drivers being little, if any, greater than had been the practice with the old plan of engine having a single pair of drivers. Hence, engines of eighteen and twenty tons weight were shortly introduced, and in 1844, three of twenty tons weight, with cylinders sixteen and one-half inches diameter by eighteen inches stroke, were constructed for the Western Railroad of Massachusetts, and six of eighteen tons weight, with cylinders fifteen by eighteen, and drivers forty-six inches in diameter, were built for the Philadelphia and Reading Railroad. It should be noted that three of these latter engines had iron flues. This was the first instance in which Mr. Baldwin had employed tubes of this material, although they had been previously used by others. Lap-welded iron flues were made by Morris, Tasker & Co., of Philadelphia, about 1838, and butt-welded iron tubes had previously been made by the same firm. Ross Winans, of Baltimore, had also made iron tubes by hand for locomotives of his manufacture, before 1838. The advantage found to result from the use of iron tubes, apart from their less cost, was that the tubes and boiler shell, being of the same material, expanded and contracted alike, while in the case of copper tubes, the expansion of the metal by heat varied from that of the boiler shell, and as a consequence there was greater liability to leakage at the joints with the tube sheets. The opinion prevailed largely at that time that some advantage resulted in the evaporation of water, owing to the superiority of copper as a conductor of heat. To determine this question, an experiment was tried with two of the six engines referred to above, one of which, the "Ontario," had copper flues, and another, the "New England," iron flues. In other respects they were precisely alike. The two engines were run from Richmond to Mount Carbon, August 27, 1844, each drawing a train of one hundred and one empty cars, and returning from Mount Carbon to Richmond on the following day, each with one hundred loaded cars. The quantity of water evaporated and wood consumed was noted, with the result shown in the following table:

	Up Trip, Aug. 27, 1844		Down Trip, Aug. 28, 1844	
	"Ontario" (Copper Flues)	"New England" (Iron Flues)	"Ontario" (Copper Flues)	"New England" (Iron Flues)
Time, running	9h. 7m.	7h. 41m.	10h. 44m.	8h. 19m.
Time, standing at stations	4h. 2m.	3h. 7m.	2h. 12m.	3h. 8m.
Cords of wood burned	6.68	5.50	6.94	6.00
Cubic feet of water evaporated	925.75	757.26	837.46	656.39
Ratio, cubic feet of water to a cord of wood	138.57	137.68	120.67	109.39

The conditions of the experiments not being absolutely the same in each case, the results could not of course be accepted as entirely accurate. They seemed to show, however, no considerable difference in the evaporative efficacy of copper and iron tubes.

The period under consideration was marked also by the introduction of the French & Baird stack, which proved at once to be one of the most successful spark-arresters thus far employed, and which was for years used almost exclusively wherever, as on the cotton-carrying railroads of the South, a thoroughly

effective spark-arrester was required. This stack was introduced
by Mr. Baird, then a foreman in the Works, who purchased
the patent right of what had been known as the Grimes stack,
and combined with it some of the features of the stack made
by Mr. Richard French, then Master Mechanic of the Germantown Railroad, together with certain improvements of his own.
The cone over the straight inside pipe was made with volute
flanges on its under side, which gave a rotary motion to the
sparks. Around the cone was a casing about six inches smaller
in diameter than the outside stack. Apertures were cut in the
sides of the casing, through which the sparks in their rotary
motion were discharged, and thus fell to the bottom of the space
between the straight inside pipe and the outside stack. The
opening in the top of the stack was fitted with a series of V-shaped
iron circles perforated with numerous holes, thus presenting
an enlarged area, through which the smoke escaped. The
patent right for this stack was subsequently sold to Messrs.
Radley & Hunter, and its essential principle is still used in
the Radley & Hunter stack. The Rushton wood-burning stack,
as now built, is a further improvement on the Radley & Hunter,
in that the design has been simplified, the draft obstruction
reduced, and the stack made more effective as a spark arrester.

During the year 1844 another important feature in locomotive construction—the cut-off valve—was added to Mr. Baldwin's
practice. Up to that time the valve motion had been the two
eccentrics, with the single flat hook for each cylinder. Since
1841, Mr. Baldwin had contemplated the addition of some device
allowing the steam to be used expansively, and he now added
the "half-stroke cut-off." In this device the steam chest was
separated by a horizontal plate into an upper and a lower compartment. In the upper compartment, a valve, worked by a
separate eccentric, and having a single opening, admitted steam
through a port in this plate to the lower steam chamber. The
valve rod of the upper valve terminated in a notch or hook,
which engaged with the upper arm of its rock shaft. When
thus working, it acted as a cut-off at a fixed part of the stroke,
determined by the setting of the eccentric. This was usually at
half the stroke. When it was desired to dispense with the cut-

off and work steam for the full stroke, the hook of the valve rod was lifted from the pin on the upper arm of the rock shaft by a lever worked from the footboard, and the valve rod was held in a notched rest fastened to the side of the boiler. This left the opening through the upper valve and the port in the partition plate open for the free passage of steam throughout the whole stroke. The first application of the half-stroke cut-off was made on the engine "Atlantic" (20 D), built for the Western Railroad of Massachusetts in 1844. It at once became the practice to apply the cut-off on all passenger engines, while the six- and eight-wheels-connected freight engines were, with a few exceptions, built for a time longer with the single valve admitting steam for the full stroke.

In 1845, Mr. Baldwin built three locomotives for the Royal Railroad Company of Würtemberg. They were of fifteen tons weight, on six wheels, four of them being sixty inches in diameter and coupled. The front drivers were combined by the flexible beams into a truck with the smaller leading wheels. The cylinders were inclined and outside, and the connecting rods took hold of a half-crank axle back of the firebox. It was specified that these engines should have the link motion which had shortly before been introduced in England by the Stephensons. Mr. Baldwin accordingly applied a link of a peculiar character to suit his own ideas of the device. The link was made solid, and of a truncated V-section, and the block was grooved so as to fit and slide on the outside of the link.

After building, during the years 1843, 1844 and 1845, ten four-wheels-connected engines on the plan above described, *viz.*: six wheels in all, the leading wheels and the front drivers being combined into a truck by the flexible beams, Mr. Baldwin finally adopted the present design of four drivers and a four-wheeled truck. Some of his customers who were favorable to the latter plan had ordered such machines of other builders, and Colonel Gadsden, President of the South Carolina Railroad Company, called on him in 1845 to build for that line some passenger engines of this pattern. He accordingly bought the patent right for this plan of engine of Mr. H. R. Campbell, and for the equalizing beams used between the drivers, of Messrs. Eastwick &

Harrison, and delivered to the South Carolina Railroad Company, in December, 1845, his first eight-wheeled engine with four drivers and a four-wheeled truck. This machine had cylinders thirteen and three-quarters by eighteen inches, and drivers sixty inches in diameter, with the springs between them arranged as equalizers. Its weight was fifteen tons. It had the half-crank axle, the cylinders being inside the frame but outside the smokebox. The inside-connected engine, counterweighting being as yet unknown, was admitted to be steadier in running, and hence more suitable for passenger service. With the completion of the first eight-wheeled "C" engine, Mr. Baldwin's feelings underwent a revulsion in favor of this plan, and his partiality for it became as great as had been his antipathy before. Commenting on the machine, he recorded himself as "more pleased with its appearance and action than any engine he had turned out." In addition to the three engines of this description for the South Carolina Railroad Company, a duplicate was sent to the Camden and Amboy Railroad Company, and a similar but lighter one to the Wilmington and Baltimore Railroad Company, shortly afterward. The engine for the Camden and Amboy Railroad Company, and perhaps the others, had the half-stroke cut-off.

From that time forward all of his four-wheels-connected machines were built on this plan, and the six-wheeled "C" engine was abandoned, except in the case of one built for the Philadelphia, Germantown and Norristown Railroad Company, in 1846, and this was afterward rebuilt into a six-wheels-connected machine. Three methods of carrying out the general design were, however, subsequently followed. At first the half-crank was used; then horizontal cylinders inclosed in the chimney seat and working a full-crank axle, which form of construction had been practiced at the Lowell Works; and eventually outside cylinders with outside connections.

Meanwhile, the flexible truck machine maintained its popularity for heavy freight service. All the engines thus far built on this plan had been six-wheeled, some with the rear driving axle back of the firebox, and others with it in front. The next step, following logically after the adoption of the eight-wheeled "C" engine, was to increase the size of the freight machine, and distribute the weight on eight wheels all connected, the two rear pairs being rigid in the frame, and the two front pairs combined into the flexible-beam truck. This was first done in 1846, when seventeen engines on this plan were constructed on one order for the Philadelphia and Reading Railroad Company. Fifteen of these were of twenty tons weight, with cylinders fifteen and one-half by twenty inches, and wheels forty-six inches in diameter; and two of twenty-five tons weight, with cylinders seventeen and one-quarter by eighteen inches, and drivers forty-two inches in diam-

BALDWIN EIGHT-WHEELS-CONNECTED ENGINE, 1846

eter. These engines were the first on which Mr. Baldwin placed sand boxes, and they were also the first built by him with roofs. On all previous engines the footboard had only been inclosed by a railing. On these engines for the Reading Railroad four iron posts were carried up, and a wooden roof supported by them. The engine men added curtains at the sides and front, and Mr. Baldwin on subsequent engines added sides, with sash and glass. The cab proper, however, was of New England origin, where the severity of the climate demanded it, and where it had been used previous to this period.

Forty-two engines were completed in 1846, and thirty-nine in 1847. The only novelty to be noted among them was the engine "M. G. Bright," built for operating the inclined plane on the Madison and Indianapolis Railroad. The rise of this incline was one in seventeen, from the bank of the Ohio River at Madison. The engine had eight wheels, forty-two inches in diameter, connected, and worked in the usual manner by outside inclined cylinders, fifteen and one-half inches diameter by twenty inches stroke. A second pair of cylinders, seventeen inches in diameter with eighteen inches stroke of piston was placed vertically over the boiler, midway between the furnace and smoke arch. The connecting rods, worked by these cylinders, connected with cranks on a shaft under the boiler. This shaft carried a single cog-wheel at its center, and this cog-wheel engaged with another of about twice its diameter on a second shaft adjacent to it and in the same plane. The cog-wheel on this latter shaft worked in a rack-rail placed in the center of the track. The shaft itself had its bearings in the lower ends of two vertical rods, one on each side of the boiler, and these rods were united over the boiler by a horizontal bar, which was connected by means of a

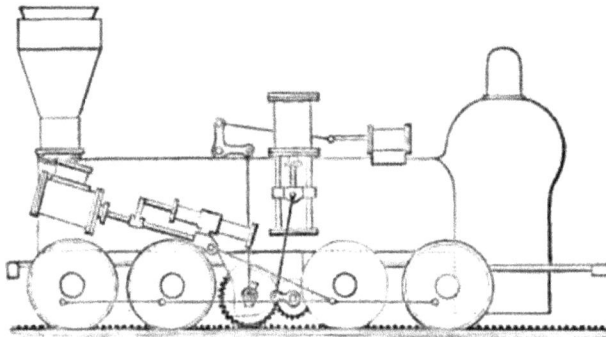

BALDWIN ENGINE FOR RACK RAIL, 1847

bent lever and connecting rod to the piston worked by a small horizontal cylinder placed on top of the boiler. By means of this cylinder, the yoke carrying the shaft and cog-wheel could be depressed and held down so as to engage the cogs with the rack-rail, or raised out of the way when only the ordinary drivers were required. This device was designed by Mr. Andrew Cathcart, Master Mechanic of the Madison and Indianapolis Railroad. A similar machine, the "John Brough," for the same plane, was built by Mr. Baldwin in 1850. The incline was worked with a rack-rail and these engines until it was finally abandoned and a line with easier gradients substituted.

The use of iron tubes in freight engines grew in favor, and in October, 1847, Mr. Baldwin noted that he was fitting his flues with copper ends, "for riveting to the boiler."

The subject of burning coal continued to engage much attention, but the use of anthracite had not as yet been generally successful. In October, 1847, the Baltimore and Ohio Railroad

Company advertised for proposals for four engines to burn Cumberland coal, and the order was taken and partially filled by Mr. Baldwin with three eight-wheels-connected machines. These engines had a heater on top of the boiler for heating the feed water, and a grate with a rocking bar in the center, having fingers on each side which interlocked with projections on fixed bars, one in front and one behind. The rocking bar was operated from the footboard. This appears to have been the first instance of the use of a rocking grate in the practice of these Works.

The year 1848 showed a falling off in business, and only twenty engines were turned out. In the following year, however, there was a rapid recovery, and the production of the Works increased to thirty, followed by thirty-seven in 1850, and fifty in 1851. These engines, with a few exceptions, were confined to three patterns: the eight-wheeled four-coupled engine, from twelve to nineteen tons in weight, for passengers and freight, and the six and eight-wheels-connected engines, for freight exclusively, the six-wheeled machine weighing from twelve to seventeen tons, and the eight-wheeled from eighteen to twenty-seven tons. The drivers of these six- and eight-wheels-connected machines were made generally forty-two, with occasional variations up to forty-eight inches in diameter.

The exceptions referred to above were the fast passenger engines built by Mr. Baldwin during this period. Early in 1848, the Vermont Central Railroad was approaching completion, and Governor Paine, the President of the Company, conceived the idea that the passenger service on the road required locomotives capable of running at very high velocities. Henry R. Campbell, Esq., was a contractor in building the line, and was authorized by Governor Paine to come to Philadelphia and offer Mr. Baldwin ten thousand dollars for a locomotive which could run with a passenger train at a speed of sixty miles per hour. Mr. Baldwin at once undertook to meet these conditions. The work was begun early in 1848, and in March of that year Mr. Baldwin filed a caveat for his design. The engine was completed in 1849, and was named the "Governor Paine." It had one pair of driving wheels, six and one-half feet in diameter, placed back of the firebox. Another pair of wheels, but smaller and unconnected, was placed directly in front of the firebox, and a four-wheeled truck carried the front of the engine. The cylinders were seventeen and one-quarter inches diameter and twenty inches stroke, and were placed horizontally between the frames and the boiler at about the middle of the waist. The connecting rods took hold of "half-cranks" inside of the driving wheels. The object of placing the cylinders at the middle of the boiler was to lessen or obviate the lateral motion of the engine, produced when the cylinders were attached to the smoke arch. The bearings on the two rear axles were so contrived that by means of a lever, a part of the weight of the engine usually carried on the wheels in front of the firebox could be transferred to the driving axle. The "Governor Paine" was

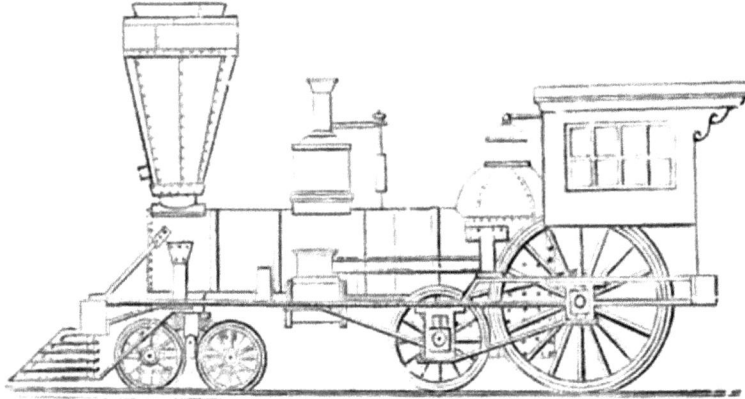

BALDWIN FAST PASSENGER ENGINE, 1848

used for several years on the Vermont Central Railroad, and then rebuilt into a four-coupled machine. During its career, it was stated by the officers of the road that it had run a mile in forty-three seconds. Three engines on the same plan, but with cylinders fourteen by twenty inches, and six-feet driving wheels, the "Mifflin," "Blair" and "Indiana," were also built for the Pennsylvania Railroad Company in 1849. They weighed each about forty-seven thousand pounds, distributed as follows: Eighteen thousand on the drivers, fourteen thousand on the pair of wheels in front of the firebox, and fifteen thousand on the truck. By applying the lever, the weight on the drivers could be increased to about twenty-four thousand pounds, the weight on the wheels in front of the firebox being correspondingly reduced. A speed of four miles in three minutes is recorded for them, and upon one occasion President Taylor was taken in a special train over the road by one of these machines at a speed of sixty miles an hour. One other engine of this pattern, the "Susquehanna," was built for the Hudson River Railroad Company in 1850. Its cylinders were fifteen inches diameter by twenty inches stroke, and drivers six feet in diameter. All these engines, however, were short-lived, and died of insufficient adhesion.

Eight engines, with four drivers connected and half-crank axles, were built for the New York and Erie Railroad Company in 1849, with seventeen by twenty-inch cylinders; one-half of the number with six-feet and the rest with five-feet drivers. These machines were among the last on which the half-crank axle was used. Thereafter, outside-connected engines were constructed almost exclusively.

In May, 1848, Mr. Baldwin filed a caveat for a four-cylinder locomotive, but never carried the design into execution. The first instance of the use of steel axles in the practice of the establishment occurred during the same year—a set being placed as an experiment under an engine constructed for the Pennsylvania Railroad Company. In 1850, the old form of dome boiler, which had characterized the Baldwin engine since 1834, was abandoned, and the wagon-top form substituted.

The business in 1851 had reached the full capacity of the shop, and the next year marked the completion of about an equal number of engines (forty-nine). Contracts for work extended a year ahead, and to meet the demand, the facilities in the various departments were increased, and resulted in the construction of sixty engines in 1853, and sixty-two in 1854.

At the beginning of the latter year, Mr. Matthew Baird, who had been connected with the Works since 1836, as one of its foremen, entered into partnership with Mr. Baldwin, and the style of the firm was made M. W. Baldwin & Co.

The only novelty in the general plan of engines during this period was the addition of a ten-wheeled engine to the patterns of the establishment. The success of Mr. Baldwin's engines with all six or eight wheels connected, and the two front pairs combined by the parallel beams into a flexible truck, had been so marked that it was natural that he should oppose any other plan for freight service. The ten-wheeled engine, with six drivers connected, had, however, now become a competitor. This plan of engine was first patented by Septimus Norris, of Philadelphia, in 1846, and the original design was apparently to produce an engine which should have equal tractive power with the Baldwin six-wheels-connected machine. This the Norris patent sought to accomplish by proposing an engine with six drivers connected, and so disposed as to carry substantially the whole weight, the forward drivers being in advance of the center of gravity of the engine, and the truck only serving as a guide, the front of the engine being connected with it by a pivot pin, but without a bearing on the center plate. Mr. Norris's first engine on this plan was tried in April, 1847, and was found not to pass curves as readily as was expected. As the truck carried little or no weight, it would not keep the track. The New York and Erie Railroad Company, of which John Brandt was then Master Mechanic, shortly afterward adopted the ten-wheeled engine, modified in plan so as to carry a part of the weight on the truck. Mr. Baldwin filled an order for this company, in 1850, of four eight-wheels-connected engines, and in making the contract he agreed to substitute a truck for the front pair of wheels if desired after trial. This, however, he was not called upon to do.

In February, 1852, Mr. J. Edgar Thomson, President of the Pennsylvania Railroad Company, invited proposals for a number of freight locomotives of fifty-six thousand pounds weight each. They were to be adapted to burn bituminous coal, and to have six wheels connected and a truck in front, which might be either of two or four wheels. Mr. Baldwin secured the contract, and built twelve engines of the prescribed dimensions, viz.: cylinders eighteen by twenty-two; drivers forty-four inches diameter, with chilled tires. Several of these engines were constructed with a single pair of truck wheels in front of the drivers, but back of the cylinders. It was found, however, after the engines were put in service, that the two truck wheels carried eighteen or nineteen thousand pounds, and this was objected to by the company as too great a weight to be carried on a single pair of wheels. On the rest of the engines of the order, therefore, a four-wheeled truck in front was employed.

The ten-wheeled engine thereafter assumed a place in the Baldwin classification, but it was not until after 1860 that this type wholly superseded Mr. Baldwin's old plan of freight engine on six or eight wheels, all connected.

In 1855-56, two locomotives of twenty-seven tons weight, with nineteen by twenty-two inch cylinders and forty-eight inch drivers, were built for the Portage Railroad, and three for the Pennsylvania Railroad. In 1855, '56 and '57, fourteen of the same dimensions were built for the Cleveland and Pittsburg Railroad; four for the Pittsburg, Fort Wayne and Chicago Railroad; and one for the Marietta and Cincinnati Railroad. In 1858 and '59, one was constructed for the South Carolina Railroad, of the same size, and six lighter ten-wheelers, with cylinders fifteen and one-half by twenty-two inches, and four-feet drivers, and two with cylinders sixteen by twenty-two inches, and four-feet drivers were sent out to railroads in Cuba.

On three locomotives—the "Clinton," "Athens," and "Sparta"—completed for the Central Railroad of Georgia in July, 1852, the driving boxes were made with a slot or cavity in the line of the vertical bearing on the journal. The object was to produce a more uniform distribution of the wear over the entire surface of the bearing. This was the first instance in which this device, which has since come into general use, was employed in the Works, and the boxes were so made by direction of Mr. Charles Whiting, then Master Mechanic of the Central Railroad of Georgia. He subsequently informed Mr. Baldwin that this method of fitting up driving boxes had been in use on the road for several years previous to his connection with the company. As this device was subsequently made the subject of a patent by Mr. David Matthew, these facts may not be without interest.

In 1853, Mr. Charles Ellet, Chief Engineer of the Virginia Central Railroad, laid a temporary track across the Blue Ridge, at Rock Fish Gap, for use during the construction of a tunnel through the mountain. This track was twelve thousand five hundred feet in length on the eastern slope, ascending in that distance six hundred and ten feet, or at the average rate of one

in twenty and one-half feet.   The maximum grade was calculated
for two hundred and ninety-six feet per mile, and prevailed for
half a mile.   It was found, however, in fact, that the grade in
places exceeded three hundred feet per mile.   The shortest radius
of curvature was two hundred and thirty-eight feet.   On the
western slope, which was ten thousand six hundred and fifty
feet in length, the maximum grade was two hundred and eighty
feet per mile, and the ruling radius of curvature three hundred
feet.   This track was worked by two of the Baldwin six-wheels-
connected flexible-beam truck locomotives constructed in 1853-
54.   From a description of this track, and the mode of working
it, published by Mr. Ellet, in 1856, the following is extracted:

"The locomotives mainly relied on for this severe duty were designed
and constructed by the firm of M. W. Baldwin & Company, of Philadelphia.
The slight modifications introduced at the instance of the writer, to adapt
them better to the particular service to be performed in crossing the Blue
Ridge, did not touch the working proportions or principle of the engines,
the merits of which are due to the patentee, M. W. Baldwin, Esq.

"These engines are mounted on six wheels, all of which are drivers,
and coupled, and forty-two inches diameter.   The wheels are set very close,
so that the distance between the extreme points of contact of the wheels
and the rail, of the front and rear drivers, is nine feet four inches.   This
closeness of the wheels, of course, greatly reduces the difficulty of turning
the short curves of the road.   The diameter of the cylinders is sixteen and
a half inches, and the length of the stroke twenty inches.   To increase the
adhesion, and at the same time avoid the resistance of a tender, the engine
carries its tank upon the boiler, and the footboard is lengthened out and provided with suspended side boxes, where a supply of fuel may be stored.
By this means the weight of wood and water, instead of abstracting from the
effective power of the engine, contributes to its adhesion and consequent
ability to climb the mountain.   The total weight of these engines is fifty-five
thousand pounds, or twenty-seven and a half tons, when the boiler and tank
are supplied with water, and fuel enough for a trip of eight miles is on board.
The capacity of the tank is sufficient to hold one hundred cubic feet of water,
and it has storage room on top for one hundred cubic feet of wood, in addition
to what may be carried in the side boxes and on the footboard.

"To enable the engines to better adapt themselves to the flexures of
the road, the front and middle pairs of drivers are held in position by wrought-
iron beams, having cylindrical boxes in each end for the journal bearings,
which beams vibrate on spherical pins fixed in the frame of the engine on each
side, and resting on the centers of the beams.   The object of this arrangement

is to form a truck, somewhat flexible, which enables the drivers more readily to traverse the curves of the road.

"The writer has never permitted the power of the engines on this mountain road to be fully tested. The object has been to work the line regularly, economically, and above all, *safely;* and these conditions are incompatible with experimental loads subjecting the machinery to severe strains. The regular daily service of each of the engines is to make four trips, of eight miles, over the mountain, drawing one eight-wheel baggage car, together with two eight-wheel passenger cars, in each direction.

"In conveying freight, the regular train on the mountain is three of the eight-wheel house cars, fully loaded, or four of them when empty or partly loaded.

"These three cars when full, weigh with their loads, from forty to orty-three tons. Sometimes, though rarely, when the business has been unusually heavy, the loads have exceeded fifty tons.

"With such trains the engines are stopped on the track, ascending or descending, and are started again, on the steepest grades, at the discretion of the engineer.

"Water for the supply of the engines has been found difficult to obtain on the mountain; and since the road was constructed a tank has been established on the eastern slope, where the ascending engines stop daily on a grade of two hundred and eighty feet per mile, and are there held by the brakes while the tank is being filled, and started again at the signal and without any difficulty.

"The ordinary speed of the engines, when loaded, is seven and a half miles an hour on the ascending grades, and from five and a half to six miles an hour on the descent.

"When the road was first opened, it speedily appeared that the difference of forty-three feet on the western side, and fifty-eight on the eastern side, between the grades on curves of three hundred feet radius and those on straight lines, was not sufficient to compensate for the increased friction due to such curvature. The velocity, with a constant supply of steam, was promptly retarded on passing from a straight line to a curve, and promptly accelerated again on passing from the curve to the straight line. But, after a little experience in the working of the road, it was found advisable to supply a small amount of grease to the flange of the engine by means of a sponge, saturated with oil, which, when needed, is kept in contact with the wheel by a spring. Since the use of the oil was introduced, the difficulty of turning the curves has been so far diminished that it is no longer possible to determine whether grades of two hundred and thirty-seven and six-tenths feet per mile on curves of three hundred feet radius, or grades of two hundred and ninety-six feet per mile on straight lines, are traversed most rapidly by the engine.

"When the track is in good condition, the brakes of only two of the cars possess sufficient power to control and regulate the movement of the train—that is to say, they will hold back the two cars and the engine. When there are three or more cars in the train, the brakes on the cars, of course, command the train so much the more easily.

"But the safety of the train is not dependent on the brakes of the car. There is also a valve or air cock in the steam chest, under the control of the engineer. This air cock forms an independent brake, exclusively at the command of the engineer, and which can always be applied when the engine itself is in working order. The action of this power may be made ever so gradual, either slightly relieving the duty of the brakes on the cars, or bringing into play the entire power of the engine. The train is thus held in complete command."

The Mountain Top Track, it may be added, was worked successfully for several years by the engines described in the above extract, until it was abandoned on the completion of the tunnel. The exceptionally steep grades and short curves which characterized the line afforded a complete and satisfactory test of the adaptation of these machines to such peculiar service.

But the period now under consideration was marked by another and a most important step in the progress of American locomotive practice. We refer to the introduction of the link motion. Although this device was first employed by William T. James, of New York, in 1832, and eleven years later by the Stephensons, in England, and was by them applied thenceforward on their engines, it was not until 1849 that it was adopted in this country. In that year Mr. Thomas Rogers, of the Rogers Locomotive and Machine Company, introduced it in his practice. Other builders, however, strenuously resisted the innovation, and none more so than Mr. Baldwin. The theoretical objections which confessedly apply to the device, but which practically have been proved to be unimportant, were urged from the first by Mr. Baldwin as arguments against its use. The strong claim of the advocates of the link motion, that it gave a means of cutting off steam at any point of the stroke, could not be gainsaid, and this was admitted to be a consideration of the first importance. This very circumstance undoubtedly turned Mr. Baldwin's attention to the subject of methods for cutting off steam, and one of the first results was his "Variable Cut-off," patented April 27, 1852. This device consisted of two valves, the upper sliding upon the lower, and worked by an eccentric and rock shaft in the usual manner. The lower valve fitted steam-tight to the sides of the steam chest and the under surface of the upper valve. When the piston reached each end of its stroke, the full pressure of steam from the boiler was admitted around the upper valve, and transferred the lower valve instantaneously from one end of the steam chest to the other. The openings through the two valves were so arranged that steam was admitted to the cylinder only for a part of the stroke. The effect was, therefore, to cut off steam at a given point, and to open the induction and exhaust ports substantially at the same instant and to their full extent. The exhaust port, in addition, remained fully opened while the induction port was gradually closing, and after it had entirely closed. Although this device was never put in use, it may be noted in passing that it contained substantially the principle of the steam pump, as since patented and constructed.

Early in 1853 Mr. Baldwin abandoned the half-stroke cut-off previously described, and which he had been using since 1845, and adopted the variable cut-off, which was already employed by other builders. One of his letters, written in January, 1853, states his position as follows:

"I shall put on an improvement in the shape of a variable cut-off, which can be operated by the engineer while the machine is running, and which will cut off anywhere from six to twelve inches, according to the load and amount of steam wanted, and this without the link motion, which I could never be entirely satisfied with. I still have the independent cut-off, and the additional machinery to make it variable will be simple and not liable to be deranged."

This form of cut-off was a separate valve, sliding on a partition plate between it and the main steam valve, and worked by an independent eccentric and rock shaft. The upper arm of the rock shaft was curved so as to form a radius arm, on which a sliding block, forming the termination of the upper valve rod, could be adjusted and held at varying distances from the axis, thus producing a variable travel of the upper valve. This device did not give an absolutely perfect cut-off, as it was not operative in backward gear, but when running forward it would cut off with great accuracy at any point of the stroke, was quick in its movement, and economical in the consumption of fuel.

After a short experience with this arrangement of the cut-off, the partition plate was omitted, and the upper valve was made to slide directly on the lower. This was eventually found objectionable, however, as the lower valve would soon cut a hollow in the valve face. Several unsuccessful attempts were made to remedy this defect by making the lower valve of brass, with long bearings, and making the valve face of the cylinder of hardened steel; finally, however, the plan of one valve on the other was abandoned, and recourse was again had to an interposed partition plate, as in the original half-stroke cut-off.

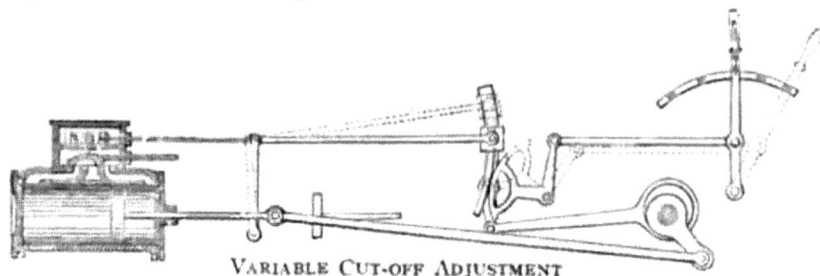

VARIABLE CUT-OFF ADJUSTMENT

Mr. Baldwin did not adopt this form of cut-off without some modification of his own, and the modification in this instance consisted of a peculiar device, patented September 13, 1853, for raising and lowering the block on the radius arm. A quadrant was placed so that its circumference bore nearly against a curved arm projecting down from the sliding block, and which curved in the reverse direction from the quadrant. Two steel straps, side by side, were interposed between the quadrant and this curved arm. One of the straps was connected to the lower end of the quadrant and the upper end of the curved arm; the other, to the upper end of the quadrant and the lower end of the curved arm. The effect was the same as if the quadrant and arm geared into each other in any position by teeth, and theoretically the block was kept steady in whatever position placed on the radius arm of the rock shaft. This was the object sought to be accomplished, and was stated in the specification of the patent as follows:

"The principle of varying the cut-off by means of a vibrating arm and sliding pivot block has long been known, but the contrivances for changing the position of the block upon the arm have been very defective. The radius of motion of the link by which the sliding block is changed on the arm, and the radius of motion of that part of the vibrating arm on which the block is placed, have, in this kind of valve gear, as heretofore constructed, been different, which produced a continual rubbing of the sliding block upon the arm while the arm is vibrating; and as the block, for the greater part of the time, occupies one position on the arm, and only has to be moved toward either extremity occasionally, that part of the arm on which the block is most used soon becomes so worn that the block is loose, and jars."

This method of varying the cut-off was first applied on the engine "Belle," delivered to the Pennsylvania Railroad Company, December 6, 1854, and thereafter was for some time employed by Mr. Baldwin. It was found, however, in practice, that the steel straps would stretch sufficiently to allow them to buckle and break, and hence they were soon abandoned, and chains substituted between the quadrant and curved arm of the sliding block. These chains in turn proved little better, as they lengthened, allowing lost motion, or broke altogether, so that eventually the quadrant was wholly abandoned, and recourse was finally had to the lever and link for raising and lowering the sliding block. As thus arranged, the cut-off was substantially what was known as the "Cuyahoga Cut-off," as introduced by Mr. Ethan Rogers, of the Cuyahoga Works, Cleveland, Ohio, except that Mr. Baldwin used a partition plate between the upper and the lower valve.

But while Mr. Baldwin in common with many other builders, was thus resolutely opposing the link motion, it was nevertheless rapidly gaining favor with railroad managers. Engineers and master mechanics were everywhere learning to admire its simplicity, and were manifesting an enthusiastic preference for engines so constructed. At length, therefore, he was forced to succumb; and the link was applied to the "Pennsylvania," one of two engines completed for the Central Railroad of Georgia, in February, 1854. The other engine of the order, the "New Hampshire," had the variable cut-off, and Mr. Baldwin, while yielding to the demand in the former engine, was undoubtedly sanguine that the working of the latter would demonstrate the inferiority of the new device. In this, however, he was disappointed, for in the following year the same company ordered three more engines, on which they specified the link motion. In 1856 seventeen engines for nine different companies had this form of valve gear, and its use was thus incorporated in his practice. It was not, however, until 1857 that he was induced to adopt it exclusively.

February 14, 1854, Mr. Baldwin and Mr. David Clark, Master Mechanic of the Mine Hill Railroad, took out conjointly a patent for a feed-water heater, placed at the base of a locomotive chimney, and consisting of one large vertical flue, surrounded by a number of smaller ones. The exhaust steam was discharged from the nozzles through the large central flue, creating a draft of the products of combustion through the smaller surrounding flues. The pumps forced the feed water into the chamber around these flues, whence it passed to the boiler by a pipe from the back of the stack. This heater was applied on several engines for the Mine Hill Railroad, and on a few other roads; but its use was exceptional, and lasted only for a year or two.

In December of the same year, Mr. Baldwin filed a caveat for a variable exhaust, operated automatically by the pressure of steam, so as to close when the pressure was lowest in the boiler, and open with the increase of pressure. The device was never put in service.

The use of coal, both bituminous and anthracite, as a fuel for locomotives, had by this time become a practical success. The economical combustion of bituminous coal, however, engaged considerable attention. It was felt that much remained to be accomplished in consuming the smoke and deriving the maximum of useful effect from the fuel. Mr. Baird, who was now associated with Mr. Baldwin in the management of the business, made this matter a subject of careful study and investigation. An experiment was conducted under his direction, by placing a sheet iron deflector in the firebox of an engine on the Germantown and Norristown Railroad. The success of the trial was such as to show conclusively that a more complete combustion resulted. As, however, a deflector formed by a single plate of iron would soon be destroyed by the action of the fire, Mr. Baird proposed to use a water-leg projecting upward and backward from the front of the firebox under the flues. Drawings and a model of the device were prepared, with a view of patenting it, but subsequently the intention was abandoned, Mr. Baird concluding that a firebrick arch as a deflector to accomplish the same object was preferable. This was accordingly tried on two locomotives built for the Pennsylvania Railroad Company in 1854, and was found so valuable an appliance that its use was at once established, and it was put on a number of engines built for railroads in Cuba and elsewhere. For several years the firebricks were supported on side plugs; but in 1858, in the "Media," built for the West Chester and Philadelphia Railroad Company, water-pipes extending from the crown obliquely downward and curving to the sides of the firebox at the bottom, were successfully used for the purpose.

The adoption of the link motion may be regarded as the dividing line between the present and the early and transitional stage of locomotive practice. Changes since that event have been principally in matters of detail, but it is the gradual perfection of these details which has made the locomotive the symmetrical, efficient, and wonderfully complete piece of mechanism it is today.

The production of the establishment during the six years from 1855 to 1860, inclusive, was as follows: forty-seven engines in 1855; fifty-nine in 1856; sixty-six in 1857; thirty-three in 1858; seventy in 1859; and eighty-three in 1860. The greater number of these were of the ordinary type: four drivers coupled, and a four-wheeled truck, and varying in weight from fifteen-ton engines, with cylinders twelve by twenty-two inches, to twenty-seven-ton engines, with cylinders sixteen by twenty-four inches. A few ten-wheeled engines were built, as has been previously noted, and the remainder were the Baldwin flexible truck six- and eight-wheels-connected engines. The demand for these, however, was now rapidly falling off, the ten-wheeled and heavy "C" engines taking their place, and by 1859 they ceased to be built, save in exceptional cases, as for some foreign roads, from which orders for this pattern were still occasionally received.

A few novelties characterizing the engines of this period may be mentioned. Several built in 1855 had cross-flues placed in the firebox, under the crown, in order to increase the heating surface. This feature, however, was found impracticable and was soon abandoned. The intense heat to which the flues were exposed converted the water contained in them into highly superheated steam, which would force its way out through the water around the firebox with violent ebullitions. Four engines, the "Tiger," "Leopard," "Hornet" and "Wasp," were built for the Pennsylvania Railroad Company, in 1856-57, with straight boilers and two domes. The "Delano" grate, by means of which the coal was forced into the firebox from below, was applied on four ten-wheeled engines for the Cleveland and Pittsburg Railroad in 1857. In 1859 several engines were built with the form of boiler introduced on the Cumberland Valley Railroad, in 1851, by Mr. A. F. Smith, and which consisted of a combustion chamber in the waist of the boiler next the firebox. This form of boiler was for some years thereafter largely used in engines for soft coal. It was at first constructed with the "water-leg" which was a vertical water space, connecting the top and bottom sheets of the combustion chamber, but eventually this feature was omitted, and an unobstructed combustion chamber employed. Several engines were built for the Philadelphia, Wilmington and Baltimore Railroad Company, in 1859 and thereafter, with the "Dimpfel" boiler, in which the tubes contain water, and starting downward from the crown sheet, are curved to the horizontal, and terminate in a narrow water space next to the smokebox. The whole waist of the boiler, therefore, forms a combustion chamber, and the heat and gases, after passing for their whole length along and around the tubes, emerge into the lower part of the smokebox.

In 1860 an engine was built for the Mine Hill Railroad, with a boiler of a peculiar form. The top sheets sloped upward from both ends toward the center, thus making a raised part or hump in the center. The engine was designed to work on heavy grades, and the object sought by Mr. Wilder, the superintendent of the Mine Hill Railroad, was to have the water always at the same height in the space from which steam was drawn, whether going up or down grade.

All these experiments are indicative of the interest then prevailing upon the subject of coal burning. The result of experience and study had meantime satisfied Mr. Baldwin that to burn soft coal successfully required no peculiar devices; that the ordinary form of boiler with plain firebox was right, with perhaps the addition of a firebrick deflector; and that the secret of the economical and successful use of coal was in the mode of firing, rather than in a different form of furnace.

The year 1861 witnessed a marked falling off in the production. The breaking out of the Civil War at first unsettled business, and by many it was thought that railroad traffic would be so largely reduced that the demand for locomotives must cease altogether. A large number of hands were discharged from the Works, and only forty locomotives were turned out during the year. It was even seriously contemplated to turn the resources of the establishment to the manufacture of shot and shell, and other munitions of war, the belief being entertained that the building of locomotives would have to be altogether suspended. So far was this from being the case, however, that after the first excitement had subsided, it was found that the demand for transportation by the General Government, and by the branches of trade and production stimulated by the war, was likely to tax the carrying capacity of the principal Northern railroads to the fullest extent. The Government itself became a large purchaser of locomotives, and it is noticeable, as indicating the increase of travel and freight transportation, that heavier machines than had ever before been built became the rule. Seventy-five engines were sent from the Works in 1862; ninety-six in 1863; one hundred and thirty in 1864; and one hundred and fifteen in 1865. During two years of this period, from May, 1862, to June, 1864, thirty-three engines were built for the United States Military Railroads.

The demand from the various coal-carrying roads in Pennsylvania and vicinity was particularly active, and large numbers of ten-wheeled engines, and of the heaviest eight-wheeled four-coupled engines, were built. Of the latter class, the majority had fifteen- and sixteen-inch cylinders; and of the former, seventeen- and eighteen-inch cylinders.

The introduction of several important features in construction marks this period. Early in 1861 four eighteen-inch cylinder freight locomotives, with six coupled wheels, fifty-two inches in diameter, and a Bissell pony truck with radius bar in front, were sent to the Louisville and Nashville Railroad Company. This was the first instance of the use of the Bissell truck in the Baldwin Works. These engines, however, were not of the regular Mogul type, as they were only modifications of the ten-wheeler, the drivers retaining the same position well back, and a pair of pony wheels on the Bissell plan taking the place of the ordinary four-wheeled truck. Other engines of the same pattern, but with eighteen and one-half inch cylinders, were built in 1862-63, for the same company, and for the Dom Pedro II. Railway of Brazil.

The introduction of steel in locomotive construction was a distinguishing feature of the period. Steel tires were first used in the Works in 1862, on some engines for the Dom Pedro II. Railway of South America. Their general adoption on American Railroads followed slowly. No tires of this material were then made in this country, and it was objected to their use that, as it took from sixty to ninety days to import them, an engine, in case of a breakage of one of its tires, might be laid up useless for several months. To obviate this objection, M. W. Baldwin & Co. imported five hundred steel tires, most of which were kept in stock, from which to fill orders. The steel tires as first used in 1862, on the locomotives for the Dom Pedro Segundo Railway, were made with a shoulder at one edge of the internal periphery, and were shrunk on the wheel centers. The accompanying sketch shows a section of the tire as then used.

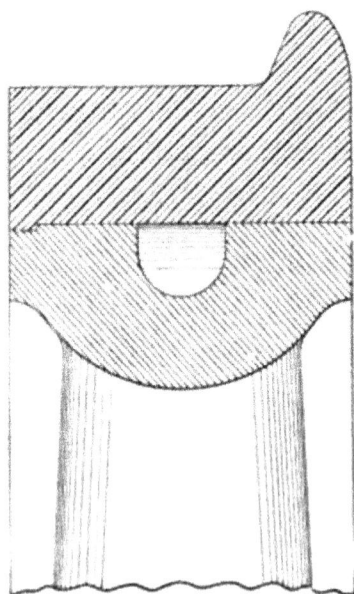

STEEL TIRE WITH SHOULDER

Steel fireboxes were first built for some engines for the Pennsylvania Railroad Company, in 1861. English steel of a high temper was used, and at the first attempt the fireboxes cracked in fitting them in the boilers, and it became necessary to take them out and substitute copper. American homogeneous cast steel was then tried on engines 231 and 232, completed for the Pennsylvania Railroad in January, 1862, and it was found to work successfully. The fireboxes of nearly all engines thereafter built for that road were of this material, and in 1866 its use for the purpose became general. It may be added that while all steel sheets for fireboxes or boilers are required to be thoroughly annealed before delivery, those which are flanged or worked in the process of boiler construction are a second time annealed before riveting.

Another feature of construction gradually adopted was the placing of the cylinders horizontally. This was first done in the case of an outside-connected engine, the "Ocmulgee," which was sent to the Southwestern Railroad Company, of Georgia, in January, 1858. This engine had a square smokebox, and the cylinders were bolted horizontally to its sides. The plan of casting the cylinder and half-saddle in one piece and fitting it to the round smokebox was introduced by Mr. Baldwin, and grew naturally out of his original method of construction. Mr. Baldwin was the first American builder to use an outside cylinder, and he made it for his early engines with a circular flange cast to it, by which it could be bolted to the boiler. The cylinders were gradually brought lower, and at a less angle, and the flanges prolonged and enlarged. In 1852, three six-wheels-connected engines, for the Mine Hill Railroad Company, were built with the cylinder flanges brought around under the smoke-box until they nearly met, the space between them being filled with a sparkbox. This was practically equivalent to making the cylinder and half-saddle in one casting. Subsequently, on other engines on which the sparkbox was not used, the half-saddles were cast so as almost to meet under the smokebox, and, after the cylinders were adjusted in position, wedges were fitted in the interstices and the saddles bolted together. It was finally discovered that the faces of the two half-saddles might be planed and finished so that they could be bolted together and bring the cylinders accurately in position, thus avoiding the trouble-some and tedious job of adjusting them by chipping and fitting to the boiler and frames. With this method of construction, the cylinders were placed at a less and less angle, until at length the truck wheels were spread sufficiently, on all new or modified classes of locomotives in the Baldwin list, to admit of the cylinders being hung horizontally, as is the present almost universal American practice. By the year 1865, horizontal cylinders were made in all cases where the patterns would allow it. The advantages of this arrangement are manifestly in the interest of simplicity and economy, as the cylinders are thus rights or lefts, indiscriminately, and a single pattern answers for either side.

In July, 1866, the engine "Consolidation" was built for the Lehigh Valley Railroad, on the plan and specification furnished by Mr. Alexander Mitchell, Master Mechanic of the Mahanoy Division of that Railroad. This engine was intended for working the Mahanoy plane, which rises at the rate of one hundred and thirty-three feet per mile. The "Consolidation" had cylinders twenty by twenty-four inches, four pairs of drivers connected, forty-eight inches in diameter, and a Bissell pony truck in front, equalized with the front drivers. The weight of the

LOCOMOTIVE "CONSOLIDATION"
Lehigh Valley R. R.

engine, in working order, was ninety thousand pounds, of which all but about ten thousand pounds was on the drivers. This engine constituted the first of a class to which it gave its name, and Consolidation engines have since been constructed for a large number of railways, not only in the United States, but also in many foreign countries. The heaviest of these locomotives weigh over three times as much as the original "Consolidation."

It has already been noted, that as early as 1839 Mr. Baldwin felt the importance of making all like parts of similar engines absolutely uniform and interchangeable. It was not attempted to accomplish this object, however, by means of a complete system of standard gauges, until many years later. In 1861 a beginning was made of organizing all the departments of manufacture upon this basis, and from it grew an elaborate and perfected system, embracing all the essential details of construction. An independent department of the Works, having a separate foreman and an adequate force of skilled workmen with special tools adapted to the purpose, is organized as the Department of Standard Gauges. A system of standard gauges and templets for every description of work to be done is made and kept by this department. The original templets are kept as "standards," and are never used on the work itself, but from them exact duplicates are made, which are issued to the foremen of the various departments, and to which all work is required to conform. The working gauges are compared with the standards at regular intervals, and absolute uniformity is thus maintained. The result of this system is interchangeableness of like parts in engines of the same class, insuring to the purchaser the minimum cost of repairs, and rendering possible, by the application of this method, the large production which these Works have accomplished.

Thus had been developed and perfected the various essential details of existing locomotive practice when Mr. Baldwin died, September 7, 1866. He had been permitted, in a life of unusual activity and energy, to witness the rise and wonderful increase of a material interest which had become the distinguishing feature of the century. He had done much, by his own mechanical skill and inventive genius, to contribute to the development of that interest. His name was as "familiar as household words" wherever on the American continent the locomotive had penetrated. An ordinary ambition might well have been satisfied with this achievement. But Mr. Baldwin's claim to the remembrance of his fellow-men rests not alone on the results of his mechanical labors. A merely technical history, such as this, is not the place to do justice to his memory as a man, as a Christian, and as a philanthropist; yet the record would be manifestly imperfect, and would fail properly to reflect the sentiments of his business associates who so long knew him in all relations of life, were no reference made to his many virtues and noble traits of character. Mr. Baldwin was a man of sterling integrity and singular conscientiousness. To do right, absolutely and unreservedly, in all his relations with men, was an instinctive rule of his nature. His heroic struggle to meet every dollar of his liabilities, principal and interest, after his failure, consequent upon the general financial crash in 1837, constitutes a chapter of personal self-denial and determined effort which is seldom paralleled in the annals of commercial experience. When most men would have felt that an equitable compromise with creditors was all that could be demanded in view of the general financial embarrassment, Mr. Baldwin insisted upon paying all claims in full, and succeeded in doing so only after nearly five years of unremitting industry, close economy, and absolute personal sacrifices. As a philanthropist and a sincere and earnest Christian, zealous in every good work, his memory is cherished by many to whom his contributions to locomotive improvement are comparatively unknown. From the earliest years of his business life the practice of systematic benevolence was made a duty and a pleasure. His liberality constantly increased with his means. Indeed, he would unhesitatingly give his notes, in large sums, for charitable purposes, when money was absolutely wanted to carry on his business. Apart from the thousands which he expended in private charities, and of which, of course, little can be known, Philadelphia contains many monuments of his munificence. Early taking a deep interest in all Christian effort, his contributions to missionary enterprise and church extension were on the grandest scale, and grew with increasing wealth. Numerous church edifices in this city, of the denomination to which he belonged, owe their existence largely to his liberality, and two at least were projected and built by him entirely at his own cost. In his mental character, Mr. Baldwin was a man of remarkable firmness of purpose. This trait was strongly shown during his mechanical career, in the persistency with which he would work at a new improvement or resist an innovation. If he were led sometimes to assume an attitude of antagonism to features of locomotive construction which after-experience showed to be valuable, (and a desire for historical accuracy has required the mention, in previous pages, of several instances of this kind) it is at least certain that his opposition was based upon a conscientious belief in the mechanical impolicy of the proposed changes.

After the death of Mr. Baldwin the business was reorganized, in 1867, under the title of "The Baldwin Locomotive Works," M. Baird & Co., proprietors. Messrs. George Burnham and Charles T. Parry, who had been connected with the establishment from an early period, the former in charge of the finances, and the latter as General Superintendent, were associated with Mr. Baird in the copartnership. Three years later Messrs. Edward H. Williams, William P. Henszey and Edward Longstreth became members of the firm. Mr. Williams had been connected with railway management on various lines since 1850. Mr. Henszey had been Mechanical Engineer, and Mr. Longstreth the General Superintendent of the Works for several years previously.

A class of engines known as Moguls, with three pairs of drivers connected, and a swinging pony truck in front equalized with the forward drivers, took its rise in the practice of this establishment from the "E. A. Douglas," built for the Thomas Iron Company in 1867. Mogul locomotives were soon extensively employed in heavy freight service on American railways, and their use continued for many years

MOGUL LOCOMOTIVE
Thomas Iron Company

after the building of the "Douglas." They have now, however, been generally replaced, in main line work, by locomotives of more powerful types. Large numbers of Mogul locomotives have been built for export, and in plantation and other forms of special service, this type is deservedly popular.

In 1867, on a number of eight-wheeled four-coupled engines for the Pennsylvania Railroad, the four-wheeled swing bolster truck was first applied, and thereafter a large number of engines have been so constructed. The two-wheeled or "pony truck" has been built both on the Bissell plan, with double inclined slides, and with the ordinary swing bolster, and in both cases with the radius bar pivoting from a point about four feet back from the center of the truck. In the case of both the two-wheeled and the four-wheeled truck, however, the swing bolster is now the rule; the four-wheeled truck being made without a radius bar. Of the engines above referred to as the first on which the swing bolster truck was applied, four were for express passenger service, with drivers sixty-seven inches in diameter, and cylinders seventeen by twenty-four inches. One of them, placed on the road September 9, 1867, was in constant service until May 14, 1871, without ever being off its wheels for repairs, making a total mileage of one hundred and fifty-three thousand two hundred and eighty miles. All of these engines had their driving wheels spread eight and one-half feet between centers.

Steel flues were first used in three ten-wheeled freight engines, numbers 211, 338 and 368, completed for the Pennsylvania Railroad in August, 1868. Steel boilers were first made in 1868 for locomotives for the Pennsylvania Railroad Company, and the use of this material for the barrels of boilers as well as for the fireboxes subsequently became universal in American practice.

In 1866, the straight boiler with two domes, first used in 1856, was again introduced; and until about 1880 the practice of the establishment included both the wagon-top boiler with single dome, and the straight boiler with one or two domes. Since 1880, the use of two domes has been exceptional, both wagon-top and straight boilers being constructed with one dome.

In 1868, a locomotive of three and one half feet gauge was constructed for the Averill Coal and Oil Company, of West Virginia. This was the first narrow gauge locomotive in the practice of the Works. In 1869, three locomotives of the same gauge were constructed for the União Valenciana Railway of Brazil and were the first narrow gauge locomotives constructed at these Works for general passenger and freight traffic. In the following year the Denver and Rio Grande Railway, of Colorado, was projected on the three-feet gauge, and the first locomotives for the line were designed and built in 1871. Two classes, for passenger and freight, respectively, were constructed. The former were six-wheeled with four wheels coupled forty inches in diameter, and nine by sixteen-inch cylinders. They weighed each, loaded, about twenty-five thousand pounds. The latter were eight-wheeled, with six wheels coupled, thirty-six inches in diameter, and eleven by sixteen-inch cylinders. These locomotives weighed each, loaded, about thirty-five thousand pounds. Both types had a swinging truck with a single pair of wheels in front of the cylinders. The six-coupled design was for freight service, and was subsequently built in larger sizes. The four-coupled type for passenger service was found to be too small and to be unsteady on the track, owing to its comparatively short wheel base. It was therefore abandoned, and the ordinary American pattern, eight-wheeled, four coupled, substituted. Following the engines for the Denver and Rio Grande Railway, others for other narrow gauge lines were called for, and the manufacture of this description of rolling stock soon assumed importance.

The Consolidation type, as first introduced for the four feet eight and one-half inches gauge in 1866, was adapted to the three feet gauge in 1873. In 1877, a locomotive on this plan, weighing in working order about sixty thousand pounds, with cylinders fifteen by twenty inches, was built for working the Garland extension of the Denver and Rio Grande Railway, which crossed the Rocky Mountains with maximum grades of two hundred and eleven feet per mile, and minimum curves of thirty degrees. The performance of this locomotive, the "Alamosa," is given in the following extract from a letter from the then General Superintendent of that railway:

DENVER, COL., August 31, 1877

"On the 29th inst. I telegraphed you from Veta Pass—Sangre de Cristo Mountains—that engine 'Alamosa' had just hauled from Garland to the Summit one baggage car and seven coaches, containing one hundred and sixty passengers. Yesterday I received your reply asking for particulars, etc.

"My estimate of the weight was eighty-five net tons, stretched over a distance of three hundred and sixty feet, or including the engine of four hundred and five feet.

"The occasion of this sized train was an excursion from Denver to Garland and return. The night before, in going over from La Veta, we had over two hundred passengers, but it was but 8 P. M., and fearing a slippery rail, I put on engine No. 19 as a pusher, although the engineer of the 'Alamosa' said he could haul the train, and I believe he could have done so. The engine and train took up a few feet more than the half circle at 'Mule Shore,' where the radius is one hundred and ninety-three feet. The engine worked splendidly, and moved up the two hundred and eleven feet grades and around the thirty degree curves seemingly with as much ease as our passenger engines on seventy-five feet grades with three coaches and baggage cars.

"The 'Alamosa' hauls regularly eight loaded cars and caboose, about one hundred net tons; length of train about two hundred and thirty feet.

"The distance from Garland to Veta Pass is fourteen and one-quarter miles, and the time is one hour and twenty minutes.

"Respectfully yours,

(Signed)   W. W. BORST, *Supt.*"

In addition to narrow gauge locomotives for the United States, this branch of the product has included a large number of three feet, meter, and three and one-half feet gauge locomotives, which have been shipped to various parts of the world.

Locomotives for single-rail railroads were built in 1878 and early in 1879, adapted respectively to the systems of General Roy Stone and Mr. W. W. Riley.

Mine locomotives, generally of narrow gauge, for underground work, and not over five and one-half feet in height, were first built in 1870. These machines were generally four-wheels-connected, with inside cylinders and a crank axle. The width over all of this plan was only sixteen inches greater than the gauge of the track. A number of outside-connected mine locomotives were also constructed, the width being thirty-two inches greater than the gauge of the track. A locomotive of twenty inches gauge for a gold mine in California was built in 1876, and was found entirely practicable and efficient.

In 1870, in some locomotives for the Kansas Pacific Railway, the steel tires were shrunk on without being secured by bolts or rivets in any form, and since that time this method of putting on tires has been usually employed.

In 1871, forty locomotives were constructed for the Ohio and Mississippi Railway, the gauge of which was changed from six feet to four feet nine inches. The entire lot of forty locomotives was completed and delivered in about twelve weeks. The gauge of the road was changed on July 4, and the forty locomotives went at once into service in operating the line on the standard gauge.

During the same year two "double-ender" locomotives of Class 10-26-¼-C were constructed for the Central Railroad of New Jersey, and were the first of this pattern at these Works.

The product of the Works, which had been steadily increasing for some years in sympathy with the requirements of the numerous new railroads which were constructing, reached three hundred and thirty-one locomotives in 1871, and four hundred and twenty-two in 1872. Orders for ninety locomotives for the Northern Pacific Railroad were entered during 1870-71, and for one hundred and twenty-four for the Pennsylvania Railroad during 1872-73, and mostly executed during those years. A contract was also made during 1872 with the Veronej-Rostoff Railway of Russia for ten locomotives to burn Russian anthracite coal. Six were Moguls, with cylinders nineteen by twenty-four inches and driving wheels four and one-half feet diameter; and four were passenger locomotives, American pattern, with cylinders seventeen by twenty-four inches, and driving wheels five and one-half feet diameter. Nine American pattern locomotives, with fifteen by twenty-four inch cylinders, and five feet driving wheels, were also constructed in 1872-73 for the Hango-Hyvinge Railway of Finland.

Early in 1873, Mr. Baird retired from the business, having sold his interest in the Works to his five partners. Mr. Baird died May 19, 1877. A new firm was formed under the style of Burnham, Parry, Williams & Co., dating from January 1, 1873, and Mr. John H. Converse, who had been connected with the Works since 1870, became a partner. The product of this year was four hundred and thirty-seven locomotives, the greatest in the history of the business up to that time. During a part of the year ten locomotives per week were turned out. Nearly three thousand men were employed. Forty-five locomotives for the Grand Trunk Railway of Canada were built in August, September and October, 1873, and all were delivered in five weeks after shipment of the first. These locomotives were built to meet the requirements of a change of gauge from five and one-half feet to four feet eight and one-half inches. In November, 1873, under circumstances of special urgency, a small locomotive for the Meier Iron Company of St. Louis, was wholly made from the raw material in sixteen working days.

The financial difficulties which prevailed throughout the United States, beginning in September, 1873, and affecting chiefly the railroad interests and all branches of manufacture connected therewith, operated, of course, to curtail the production of locomotives for quite a period. Hence, only two hundred and five locomotives were built in 1874, and one hundred and thirty in 1875. Among these may be enumerated two sample locomotives for burning anthracite coal (one passenger, sixteen by twenty-four inch cylinders, and one Mogul freight, eighteen by twenty-four inch cylinders) for the Technical Department of the Russian Government; also twelve Mogul freight locomotives, nineteen by twenty-four inch cylinders, for the Charkoff Nicolaieff Railroad of Russia. A small locomotive to work by compressed air, for drawing street cars, was constructed during 1874 for the Compressed Air Locomotive and Street Car Company, of Louisville, Ky. It had cylinders seven by twelve inches, and four wheels coupled, thirty inches in diameter. Another and smaller locomotive, to work by compressed air, was constructed three years later for the Plymouth Cordage Company, of Massachusetts, for service on a track in and about their works. It had cylinders five by ten inches, four wheels coupled, twenty-four inches diameter, and weighed seven thousand pounds; and was successfully employed for the work required.

In 1875 the Baldwin Locomotive Works acquired a controlling interest in the Standard Steel Works, located at Burnham, Pennsylvania.

The year 1876, noted as the year of the Centennial International Exhibition, in Philadelphia, brought some increase of business, and two hundred and thirty-two locomotives were constructed. An exhibit consisting of eight locomotives was prepared for this occasion. With the view of illustrating not only the different types of American locomotives, but the practice of different railroads, the exhibit consisted chiefly of locomotives constructed to fill orders from various railroad companies of the United States and from the Imperial Government of Brazil. A Consolidation locomotive for burning anthracite coal, for the Lehigh Valley Railroad, for which line the first locomotive of this type was designed and built in 1866; a similar locomotive, to burn bituminous coal, and a passenger locomotive for the same fuel for the Pennsylvania Railroad; a Mogul freight locomotive, the "Principe do Grão Pará," for the Dom Pedro Segundo Railway of Brazil, and a passenger locomotive (anthracite burner) for the Central Railroad of New Jersey, comprised the larger locomotives contributed by these Works to the Exhibition of 1876. To these were added a mine locomotive and two narrow (three feet) gauge locomotives, which were among those used in working the Centennial Narrow Gauge Railway. As this line was in many respects unique, we subjoin the following extracts from an account by its General Manager of the performance of the two three feet gauge locomotives:

"The gauge of the line was three feet, with double track three and a half miles long, or seven miles in all. For its length, it was probably the most crooked road in the world, being made up almost wholly of curves, in order to run near all the principal buildings on the Exhibition grounds. Many of these curves were on our heaviest grades, some having a radius of 215, 230 and 250 feet on grades of 140 and 155 feet per mile. These are unusually heavy grades and curves, and when *combined* as we had them, with only a thirty-five pound iron rail, made the task for our engines exceedingly difficult.

"Your locomotive 'Schuylkill,' Class 8-18-C (eight-wheeled, four wheels coupled three and a half feet diameter; cylinders, twelve by sixteen; weight, forty-two thousand six hundred and fifty pounds), began service May 13th, and made one hundred and fifty-six days to the close of the Exhibition. The locomotive 'Delaware,' Class 8-18-D (eight-wheeled, six wheels coupled three feet diameter; cylinders, twelve by sixteen; weight, thirty-nine thousand pounds), came into service June 9th, and made one hundred and thirty-one days to the close of the Exhibition. The usual load of each engine was five eight-wheeled passenger cars, frequently carrying over one hundred passengers per car. On special occasions, as many as six and seven loaded cars have been drawn by one of these engines.

"Each engine averaged fully sixteen trips daily, equal to fifty-six miles, and as the stations were but a short distance apart, the Westinghouse air brake was applied in making one hundred and sixty daily stops, or a total of twenty-five thousand for each engine. Neither engine was out of service an hour, unless from accidents for which they were in no way responsible."

[NOTE.—Average weight of each loaded car about twelve gross tons.]

The year 1876 was also marked by an extension of locomotive engineering to a new field in the practice of these Works. In the latter part of the previous year an experimental steam street car was constructed for the purpose of testing the applicability of steam to street railways. This car was completed in November, 1875, and was tried for a few days on a street railway in Philadelphia. It was then sent to Brooklyn, December 25, 1875, where it ran from that time until June, 1876. One engineer ran the car and kept it in working order. Its consumption of fuel was between seven and eight pounds of coal per mile run. It drew regularly, night and morning, an additional car, with passengers going into New York in the morning, and returning at night. On several occasions, where speed was practicable, the car was run at the rate of sixteen to eighteen miles per hour.

In June, 1876, this car was withdrawn from the Atlantic Avenue Railway of Brooklyn, and placed on the Market Street Railway of Philadelphia. It worked on that line with fair success, and very acceptably to the public, from June till nearly the close of the Centennial Exhibition.

This original steam car was built with cylinders under the body of the car, the connecting rods taking hold of a crank axle, to which the front wheels were attached. The rear wheels of the car were independent, and not coupled with the front wheels.

The machinery of the car was attached to an iron bed plate bolted directly to the wooden frame work of the car body. The experiment with this car demonstrated to the satisfaction of its builders the mechanical practicability of the use of steam on street railways, but the defects developed by this experimental car were: first, that it was difficult, or impossible, to make a crank axle which would not break, the same experience being reached in this respect which had already presented itself in locomotive construction; second, it was found that great objection existed to attaching the machinery to the wooden car body, which was not sufficiently rigid for the purpose, and which

STEAM STREET CAR

suffered by being racked and strained by the working of the machinery.

For these reasons this original steam car was reconstructed, in accordance with the experience which nearly a year's service had suggested. The machinery was made outside-connected, the same as an ordinary locomotive, and a strong iron framework was designed entirely independent of the car body, and supporting the boiler and all the machinery.

The car as thus reconstructed was named the "Baldwin," and is shown by the accompanying illustration.

The next step in this direction was the construction of a separate motor, to which one or more cars could be attached.

Such a machine, weighing about sixteen thousand pounds, was constructed in the fall of 1876, and sent to the Citizen's Railway of Baltimore, which had a maximum grade of seven feet per hundred, or three hundred and sixty-nine and six-tenths feet per mile. It ascended this grade drawing one loaded car, when the tracks were covered with mixed snow and dirt to a depth of eight to ten inches in places. Another and smaller motor, weighing only thirteen thousand pounds, was constructed about the same time for the Urbano Railway, of Havana, Cuba. Orders for other similar machines followed, and during the ensuing years, 1877-80, one hundred and seven separate motors and twelve steam cars were included in the product. Various city and suburban railways

STEAM MOTOR FOR STREET CAR

were constructed with the especial view of employing steam power, and were equipped with these machines. One line, the Hill and West Dubuque Street Railway, of Dubuque, Iowa, was constructed early in 1877, of three and one half feet gauge with a maximum gradient of nine in one hundred, and was worked exclusively by two of these motors. The details and character of construction of these machines were essentially the same locomotive work, but they were made so as to be substantially noiseless, and to show little or no smoke and steam in operation.

Steel fireboxes with vertical corrugations in the side sheets were first made by these Works early in 1876, in locomotives for the Central Railroad of New Jersey, and for the Delaware, Lackawanna and Western Railway.

The first American locomotives for New South Wales and Queens were constructed by the Baldwin Locomotive Works in 1877, and have since been succeeded by additional orders.

Six locomotives of the Consolidation type for three and one-half feet gauge were also constructed in the latter year for the Government Railways of New Zealand, and two freight locomotives, six-wheels-connected, with forward truck, for the Government of Victoria. Four similar locomotives (ten-wheeled, six coupled, with sixteen by twenty-four inch cylinders) were also built during the same year for the Norwegian State Railways.

Forty heavy Mogul locomotives (nineteen by twenty-four inch cylinders, driving wheels four and one-half feet in diameter) were constructed early in 1878 for two Russian Railways (the Koursk Charkoff Azof, and the Orel Griazi). The definite order for these locomotives was received on the sixteenth of December, 1877, and as all were required to be delivered in Russia by the following May, especial despatch was necessary. The working force was increased from eleven hundred to twenty-three hundred men in about two weeks. The first of the forty engines was erected and tried under steam on January 5th, three weeks after receipt of order, and was finished, ready to dismantle and pack for shipment, one week later. The last engine of this order was completed February 13th. The forty engines were thus constructed in about eight weeks, besides twenty-eight additional engines on other orders, which were constructed, wholly or partially, and shipped during the same period.

Four tramway motors of twelve tons weight were built early in 1879, on the order of the New South Wales Government, for a tramway having grades of six per cent., and running from the railway terminus to the Sydney Exhibition Grounds. Subsequent orders followed for additional motors for other tramways in Sydney.

The five thousandth locomotive, finished in April, 1880, presented some novel features. It was designed for fast passenger service on the Bound Brook line between Philadelphia and New York, and to run with a light train at a speed of sixty miles per hour, using anthracite coal as fuel. It had cylinders eighteen by twenty-four inches, one pair of driving wheels six and one-half feet in diameter, and a pair of trailing wheels forty-five inches in diameter, and equalized with the driving wheels. Back of the driving wheels and over the trailing wheels space was given for a wide firebox (eight feet long by seven feet wide inside) as required for anthracite coal. By an auxiliary steam cylinder placed under the waist of the boiler, just in front of the firebox, the bearings on the equalizing beams between trailing and driving wheels could be changed to a point forward of their normal position, so as to increase the weight on the driving wheels when required. The adhesion could thus be varied between the limits of thirty-five thousand and forty-five thousand pounds on the single pair of driving wheels. This feature of the locomotive was made the subject of a patent.

In 1881, a compressed air locomotive was constructed for the Pneumatic Tramway Engine Company, of New York, on plans prepared by Mr. Robert Hardie. Air tanks of steel, one-half inch thick, with a capacity of four hundred and sixty-five cubic feet, were combined with an upright cylindrical heater, thirty-two and five-eighths inches in diameter. The weight of the machine was thirty-five thousand pounds, of which twenty-eight thousand pounds were on four driving wheels, forty-two inches in diameter.

STEAM INSPECTION CAR

The cylinders were twelve and one-half inches diameter by eighteen inches stroke. Another novelty of the year was a steam car to take the place of a hand car. The accompanying illustration shows the design. Its cylinders were four by ten inches, and wheels twenty-four inches diameter. Built for standard gauge track, its weight in working order was five thousand one hundred and ten pounds. Similar cars have since been constructed.

During this year the largest single order placed on the books to that date was entered for the Mexican National Construction Company. It was for one hundred and fifty locomotives, but only a portion of them were ever built.

The year 1882 was marked by a demand for locomotives

greater than could be met by the capacity of existing locomotive works. Orders for one thousand three hundred and twenty-one locomotives were entered on the books during the year, deliveries of the greater part being promised only in the following year.

Early in 1882 an inquiry was received from the Brazilian Government for locomotives for the Cantagallo Railway, which were required to meet the following conditions: to haul a train of forty gross tons of cars and lading up a grade of eight and three-tenths per cent. (four hundred and thirty-eight feet per mile), occurring in combination with curves of forty metres radius (one hundred and thirty-one feet radius, or forty-three and eight-tenths degrees). The line was laid with heavy steel rails, to a gauge of one and one-tenth metres, or three feet seven and one-third inches. The track upon which it was proposed to run these locomotives was a constant succession of reverse curves, it being stated that ninety-one curves of the radius named occurred within a distance of three thousand four hundred and twenty-nine metres, or about two miles. The line had previously been operated on the "Fell" system, with central rack-rail, and it was proposed to introduce locomotives working by ordinary adhesion, utilizing the central rail for the application of brake power. An order was eventually received to proceed with the construction of three locomotives to do this work. The engines built were of the following general dimensions, *viz.:* cylinders, eighteen by twenty inches; six driving wheels, connected, thirty-nine inches in diameter; wheel base, nine feet six inches; boiler, fifty-four inches in diameter, with one hundred and ninety flues two inches diameter, ten feet nine inches long; and with side tanks, carried on the locomotive. In March, 1883, they were shipped from Philadelphia, and on a trial made October 17, in the presence of the officials of the road and other prominent railway officers, the guaranteed performance was accomplished. One of the engines pulled a train weighing forty tons, composed of three freight cars loaded with sleepers, and one passenger car, and made the first distance of eight kilometres to Boca do Mato with a speed of twenty-four kilometres per hour; from there it started, making easily an acclivity of eight and five-tenths per cent. in grade, and against a curve of forty metres in radius. Eight additional locomotives for this line were constructed at intervals during the following ten years, and the road has been worked by adhesion locomotives since their adoption as above described.

In 1885 a locomotive was built for the Dom Pedro Segundo Railway of Brazil, having five pairs of driving wheels connected, and a leading two-wheeled truck. From this has arisen the title "Decapod" (having ten feet) as applied to subsequent locomotives of this type. Its cylinders were twenty-two by twenty-six inches; driving wheels forty-five inches diameter, and grouped in a driving wheel base of seventeen feet. The rear flanged driving wheels, however, were given one-quarter of an inch more total play on the rails than the next adjacent pair; the second

DECAPOD LOCOMOTIVE
For the Dom Pedro Segundo Railway of Brazil

and third pairs were without flanges, and the front pair was flanged. The locomotive could therefore pass a curve of a radius as short as five hundred feet, the rails being spread one-half inch wider than the gauge of track, as is usual on curves. The flanges of the first and fourth pairs of driving wheels making practically a rigid wheel base of twelve feet eight inches, determined the friction on a curve. The weight of the engine, in working order, was one hundred and forty-one thousand pounds, of which one hundred and twenty-six thousand pounds were on the driving wheels. During this year the first rack-rail locomotive in the practice of these Works was constructed for the Ferro Principe do Grão Pará Railroad of Brazil. Its general dimensions were: cylinders, twelve by twenty inches; pitch line of cog-wheel, forty-one and thirty-five one-hundredths inches; weight, fifteen and seventy-four one-hundredths tons. Several additional similar locomotives, but of different weights, have since been constructed for the same line.

At the close of this year Mr. Edward Longstreth withdrew from the firm on account of ill health, and a new partnership was formed, adding Messrs. William C. Stroud, William H. Morrow, and William L. Austin. Mr. Stroud had been connected with the business since 1867, first as bookkeeper, and subsequently as Financial Manager. Mr. Morrow, since entering the service in 1871, had acquired a varied and valuable experience, first in the accounts, then in the department of extra work, and subsequently as Assistant Superintendent, becoming General Manager on Mr. Longstreth's retirement. Mr. Austin, who entered the works in 1870, had for several years been assistant to Mr. Henszey in all matters connected with the designing of locomotives.

On February 11, 1886, Mr. S. M. Vauclain, who had been connected with the Works since 1883, was appointed General Superintendent. The retirement of Mr. Longstreth was necessarily followed by a number of changes in the organization. Mr. Edwin W. Heald, who had been assisting Mr. Longstreth and was in line for promotion to the position of General Superintendent, was unable to assume the duties of the office on account of poor health, hence Mr. Vauclain's appointment.

A locomotive for the Antofogasta Railway (thirty inches gauge) of Chili, constructed with outside frames, was completed

LOCOMOTIVE WITH OUTSIDE FRAMES
For the Antofogasta Railway, Chili

in November, 1886, and is shown by the illustration herewith. The advantages of this method of construction of narrow gauge locomotives in certain cases were evidenced in the working of this machine, in giving a greater width of firebox between the frames, and a greater stability of the engine due to the outside journal bearings.

In 1887, a new form of boiler was brought out in some ten-wheeled locomotives constructed for the Denver and Rio Grande Railroad. A long wagon-top was used, extending sufficiently forward of the crown sheet to allow the dome to be placed in front of the firebox and near the center of the boiler, and the crown sheet was supported by radial stays from the outside shell. Many boilers of this type have since been constructed.

Mr. Charles T. Parry, who had been connected with the Works almost from their beginning, and a partner since 1867, died on July 18, 1887, after an illness of several months.

The first locomotives for Japan were shipped in June, 1887. These were two six-wheeled engines of three feet six inches gauge for the Mie Kie mines.

Mr. William H. Morrow, a partner since January 1, 1886, and who had been previously associated with the business since 1871, died February 19, 1888.

The demand for steam motors for street railway service attained large proportions at this period, and ninety-five were built during the years 1888 and 1889. Two rack-rail locomotives on the Riggenbach system, one with a single cog-wheel and four carrying wheels, and weighing in working order thirty-two thousand pounds, for the Corcovado Railway of Brazil, and the other having two cog-wheels

RACK LOCOMOTIVE, RIGGENBACH SYSTEM

and eight carrying wheels, and weighing in working order seventy-nine thousand pounds, for the Estrada de Ferro Principe do Grão Pará of Brazil, were constructed during this year. Illustrations of these locomotives are presented herewith.

The ten thousandth locomotive was built in June, 1889, for the Northern Pacific Railroad. This locomotive had twenty-two by twenty-eight inch cylinders, and weighed one hundred and forty-seven thousand five hundred pounds in working order. It was representative of the heaviest class of Consolidation locomotive built at that time.

In October, 1889, the first compound locomotive in the practice of the Works was completed and placed on the Baltimore and Ohio Railroad. It was of the four-cylinder type, as designed and patented by Mr. S. M. Vauclain. The economy in fuel and water and the efficiency of this design in both passenger and freight service led to its introduction on many leading railroads, and Vauclain compound locomotives were built in large numbers during the fifteen years following the construction of the first one.

RACK LOCOMOTIVE WITH TWO COG-WHEELS

In 1889 a test case was made to see in how short a time a locomotive could be built. On June 22d, Mr. Robert Coleman ordered a narrow gauge locomotive of the American type, which was to be ready for service on his railroad in Lebanon County, Pa., by July 4th following. The locomotive was actually completed on July 2d, having been built from the raw material in eight working days.

The manufacture of wrought iron wheel centers for both truck and driving wheels was begun at this time under patents of Mr. S. M. Vauclain, Nos. 462,605, 462,606 and 531,487.

During the year 1890, the Erecting Shop, which fronted on Broad Street, adjoining the main office, was entirely reconstructed. The new shop was a single-story building, 42 feet high to the eaves, and measuring 160 feet wide by 337 feet long. It contained nineteen tracks, each capable of accommodating four locomotives. All the machinery in the shop was driven by electric motors, and material was handled by two electric travelling cranes of 100 tons capacity each. This is the first instance on record of a shop being electrically equipped throughout.

In 1890 the first rack-rail locomotive on the Abt system was constructed for the Pike's Peak Railroad, and during this year and 1893 four locomotives were built for working the grades of that line, which vary from eight to twenty-five per cent. One of these locomotives, weighing in working order fifty-two thousand six hundred and eighty pounds, pushes twenty-five thousand pounds up the maximum grades of one in four. An illustration is here given of one of these locomotives, which is a four-cylinder compound.

RACK LOCOMOTIVE, ABT SYSTEM

Three Mogul locomotives, of one metre gauge, fifteen by eighteen inch cylinders, driving wheels forty-one inches diameter, were completed and shipped in July, 1890, for working the Jaffa and Jerusalem Railway in Palestine, and two additional locomotives for the same line were constructed in 1892.

In 1891 the name of the firm was changed to Burnham, Williams & Co., the partners being George Burnham, Edward H. Williams, William P. Henszey, John H. Converse, William C. Stroud, and William L. Austin.

In 1891 the largest locomotives in the practice of the Works, to that date, were designed and constructed for the St. Clair Tunnel of the Grand Trunk Railway, under the St. Clair River.

TEN COUPLED TANK LOCOMOTIVE

Four tank locomotives were supplied, each with cylinders twenty-two by twenty-eight inches; five pairs of driving wheels connected, fifty inches diameter; and side tanks of twenty-one hundred gallons capacity. The weight in working order of each engine was one hundred and eighty-six thousand eight hundred pounds without fire in the firebox. The tunnel is six thousand feet long, with grades of two per cent. at each entrance, twenty-five hundred, and nineteen hundred and fifty feet long respectively. Each locomotive was required to take a train load of seven hundred and sixty tons exclusive of its own weight, and in actual operation each of these locomotives has hauled from twenty-five to thirty-three loaded cars in one train through the tunnel.

For the New York, Lake Erie and Western Railroad, five compound locomotives of the Decapod class were completed in December, 1891. Their general dimensions were as follows: cylinders, high-pressure sixteen inches, low-pressure twenty-seven inches diameter, stroke twenty-eight inches; five pairs of driving wheels coupled, fifty inches diameter, in a wheel base of eighteen feet ten inches; boiler, seventy-six inches diameter, of the Wootten type; weight in working order, one hundred and ninety-five thousand pounds; and weight on driving wheels, one hundred and seventy-two thousand pounds. The first, fourth and fifth pairs of driving wheels were flanged, but the fifth pair had one-fourth inch additional play on the track. These locomotives were used as pushers on the Susquehanna Hill, where curves of five degrees are combined with grades of sixty feet per mile, doing the work of two ordinary Consolidation locomotives. From one thousand two hundred and fifty to one thousand three hundred net tons of cars and lading, making a train of forty-five loaded cars, were hauled by one of these locomotives in connection with a twenty by twenty-four inch cylinder Consolidation.

RACK-RAIL LOCOMOTIVE FOR ITALY

Mr. William C. Stroud, who had been a partner since 1886, died on September 21, 1891.

The first locomotives for Africa were constructed during this year. They were of the Mogul type, with cylinders eighteen by twenty-two inches, driving wheels forty-eight inches diameter, and of three feet six inches gauge.

The product of 1892 and 1893 included, as novelties, two rack-rail locomotives for a mountain railway near Florence,

Italy, and twenty-five compound Forney locomotives for the South Side Elevated Railroad of Chicago. At the World's Columbian Exposition in Chicago, May to October, 1893, inclusive, an exhibit was made, consisting of seventeen locomotives, as follows:

STANDARD GAUGE.—A Decapod locomotive, similar to those previously described, built in 1891 for the New York, Lake Erie and Western Railroad. A high-speed locomotive of new type, with Vauclain compound cylinders, a two-wheeled leading truck, two pairs of driving wheels, and a pair of trailing wheels under the firebox. This locomotive was named "Columbia," and the same name has been applied to the type. An express passenger locomotive of the pattern used by the Central Railroad of New Jersey; one of the pattern used by the Philadelphia and Reading Railroad, and one of the pattern used by the Baltimore and Ohio Railroad. The three roads mentioned together operated the "Royal Blue Line" between New York and Washington. A saddle tank double-ender type locomotive, with steam windlass, illustrating typical logging locomotive practice. A single expansion American type locomotive with cylinders eighteen by twenty-four inches. A single expansion Mogul locomotive with cylinders nineteen by twenty-four inches. A single expansion ten-wheeled freight locomotive with cylinders twenty by twenty-four inches, for the Baltimore and Ohio Southwestern Railroad. A compound ten-wheeled passenger locomotive shown in connection with a train exhibited by the Pullman Car Company. A compound Consolidation locomotive for the Norfolk and Western Railroad.

Three locomotives were shown in connection with the special exhibit of the Baltimore and Ohio Railroad, *viz.:* one compound, one single-expansion, and one ten-wheeled passenger locomotive.

NARROW GAUGE.—A metre gauge compound American type locomotive; a three feet gauge ten-wheeled compound locomotive with outside frames, for the Mexican National Railroad; and a thirty inch gauge saddle tank locomotive for mill or furnace work.

The depression of business which began in the summer of 1893, reduced the output of the Works for that year to seven

hundred and seventy-two, and in 1894 to three hundred and
thirteen locomotives. Early in 1895, a new type of passenger
locomotive, illustrated herewith, was brought out for the Atlantic
Coast Line. To this the name "Atlantic" type was given. The
advantages of this design are a large boiler, fitting the engine for

ATLANTIC TYPE LOCOMOTIVE

high speed; a firebox of liberal proportions and of desirable
form placed over the rear frames, and having ample depth
and width; and the location of the driving wheels in front of
the firebox, allowing the boiler to be placed lower than in the
ordinary American or Ten-wheeled type. For the enginemen,
who, in this class of locomotive, ride behind, instead of over the
driving wheels, greater ease in riding, and greater safety in case
of the breakage of a side-rod, are important advantages.

The first electric locomotive was constructed in 1895, and
was intended for experimental work for account of the North
American Company. The
electrical parts were
designed by Messrs.
Sprague, Duncan &
Hutchison, Electrical En-
gineers, New York. Two
other electric locomotives
for use in connection with
mining operations were
built in 1896, in co-opera-

ELECTRIC LOCOMOTIVE

tion with the Westinghouse Electric and Manufacturing Company, which supplied the electrical parts.

A high speed passenger locomotive, embracing several novel
features, was built in 1895, for service on the New York division

of the Philadelphia and Reading Railroad. The boiler was of the Wootten type, the cylinders were compound, thirteen and twenty-two by twenty-six inches, and the driving wheels (one pair) were eighty-four and one-quarter inches diameter. The cut below shows the general design.

The weight of the engine in working order was as follows: On front truck, thirty-nine thousand pounds; on trailing wheels, twenty-eight thousand pounds; on the driving wheels, forty-eight thousand pounds. This locomotive and a duplicate built in the following year were regularly used in passenger service,

HIGH SPEED LOCOMOTIVE
For the Philadelphia and Reading Railway

hauling five cars and making the distance between Jersey City and Philadelphia, ninety miles, in one hundred and five minutes, including six stops.

In July, 1895, a combination rack and adhesion locomotive was constructed for the San Domingo Improvement Company. This locomotive was designed by Messrs. Wm. P. Henszey and S. M. Vauclain, and was made the subject of a patent. It had compound cylinders eight inches and thirteen inches diameter by eighteen inches stroke to operate two pairs of coupled adhesion wheels, and a pair of single expansion cylinders, eleven inches by eighteen inches, to operate a single rack wheel constructed upon the Abt system. It was furnished with two complete sets of machinery, entirely independent of each other,

COMBINATION RACK AND ADHESION LOCOMOTIVE
For the San Domingo Improvement Co.

and was built with the view eventually to remove the rack attachments and operate the locomotive by adhesion alone.

During the years 1895 and 1896 contracts were executed for several railroads in Russia, aggregating one hundred and thirty-eight locomotives of the four-cylinder compound type.

COMBINATION RACK AND ADHESION LOCOMOTIVE
For the Peñoles Mining Co.

On January 1, 1896, Messrs. Samuel M. Vauclain, Alba B. Johnson, and George Burnham, Jr., were admitted to partnership.

Two combination rack and adhesion locomotives, for the Peñoles Mining Company of Mexico, were built in 1896, having compound cylinders nine and one-half and fifteen inches diameter by twenty-two inches stroke, connected to the driving wheels through walking beams.

Each locomotive had three coupled axles, which carried rack pinions of the Abt system. When operating on the rack section of the line, all the wheels ran loose on the axles, and acted as

CLUTCH USED ON LOCOMOTIVE FOR PEÑOLES MINING CO.

carrying wheels only. When, however, it was necessary to propel the locomotive by adhesion alone, two pairs of wheels could be secured to their respective axles, and thus made to turn with them, by means of clutches. These clutches were controlled by a hand lever placed in the cab. This device was made the subject of a patent, which was granted to Messrs. S. M. Vauclain and J. Y. McConnell. The drawing of the clutch mechanism on page 84 is reproduced from the patent specification.

In the latter part of the year 1896, six locomotives were built for the Baltimore and Ohio Railroad, for express passenger service. One of these locomotives, No. 1312, is here illustrated. They were of the Ten-wheeled type, with cylinders twenty-one by twenty-six inches, driving wheels seventy-eight inches diameter, and weighed each, in working order, about one hundred and

TEN-WHEELED LOCOMOTIVE
For Baltimore and Ohio Railroad

forty-five thousand pounds, about one hundred and thirteen thousand pounds of which were on the driving wheels. These locomotives handled the fast passenger trains on the Baltimore and Ohio Railroad running between Philadelphia, Baltimore and Washington with great efficiency for about fifteen years, when they were replaced by heavier power.

Early in 1897, a group of unusually interesting locomotives were shipped to the Nippon Railway (Japan). These locomotives were all designed to burn a most inferior quality of coal, requiring large grate area and a firebox of ample depth and volume. They were of two types—the Atlantic, for passenger service, and a modified design of Consolidation for freight service. The latter had a wide, deep firebox, which was placed entirely back of the driving wheels and over a rear truck. The accompanying illustration represents the design. All these locomotives proved highly successful. Freight locomotives of a design similar to those built for the Nippon Railway, were subsequently introduced in the United States, and were appropriately designated the "Mikado" type.

THE FIRST MIKADO TYPE LOCOMOTIVE BUILT FOR THE NIPPON RAILWAY

In the summer of 1897, the Reading Railway placed a fast train on its Atlantic City Division, allowing fifty-two minutes for running time from Camden to Atlantic City, a distance of fifty-five and one-half miles, making the average rate of speed sixty-four miles per hour. The trains averaged five and six cars, having a total weight of about two hundred tons, not including the engine and tender. This train was hauled by a locomotive of the Atlantic type, having Vauclain compound cylinders, thirteen and twenty-two inches in diameter by twenty-six inches stroke, with driving wheels eighty-four and one-quarter inches in diameter. The weight in working order on driving wheels was

ATLANTIC TYPE LOCOMOTIVE
For Philadelphia and Reading Railway

seventy-eight thousand six hundred pounds, the total weight of engine and tender complete being two hundred and twenty-seven thousand pounds. The records show that for fifty-two days from

July 2d to August 31, 1897, the average time consumed on the run was forty-eight minutes, equivalent to a uniform rate of speed from start to stop of sixty-nine miles per hour. On one occasion the distance was covered in forty-six and one-half minutes, an average of seventy-one and six-tenths miles per hour. The Railway Company's official record of the train for the season is reproduced on the following page. The service proved so popular that additional trains, making equally high speed, were subsequently established.

In 1898, the first cast steel frames used by the Baldwin Locomotive Works were applied to a consignment of Consolidation locomotives built for the Atchison, Topeka and Santa Fe Railway Company.

In November, 1898, a locomotive was built for the Lehigh Valley Railroad for use on the mountain cut-off between Coxton and Fairview, near Wilkesbarre. This locomotive was of the Consolidation type, with Vauclain compound cylinders, and of the following general dimensions: cylinders, eighteen and thirty inches diameter, thirty inches stroke; driving wheels, fifty-five inches outside diameter; weight in working order, on drivers, two hundred and two thousand two hundred and thirty-two pounds; weight, total engine, two hundred and twenty-six thousand pounds; weight of engine and tender about three hundred and forty-six thousand pounds. This locomotive was

CONSOLIDATION LOCOMOTIVE
For Lehigh Valley Railroad

guaranteed to haul a load of one thousand net tons exclusive of the weight of the engine and tender, on a grade of sixty-six feet per mile, at an average speed of seventeen miles per hour. It fulfilled this guarantee and fourteen similar locomotives were subsequently ordered by this Company.

Performance of Train No. 25 for July and August, 1897

Copy of Train Despatcher's sheet, showing exact running time of train, to which is added a statement showing number of cars in train, number of passengers carried and average number of miles per hour for each trip

LOCOMOTIVE 1027

JULY

Stations	Distance	Schd. Time	2d	3d	6th	7th	8th	9th	10th	12th	13th	14th	15th	16th	17th	18th	19th	20th	21st	22d	23d	24th	26th	27th	28th	29th	30th	61st
Camden	.0	3.48	3.50	3.50	3.50	3.51	3.50	3.49	3.49	3.49	3.49	3.49	3.50	3.51	3.51	3.51	3.51	3.51	3.50	3.50	3.49	3.49	3.49	3.49	3.48	3.49	3.49	3.50
West Collingswood	3.1	3.54	3.55	3.55	3.55	3.56	3.55	3.55	3.54	3.54	3.54	3.54	3.54	3.55	3.55	3.56	3.55	3.55	3.56	3.55	3.54	3.54	3.54	3.54	3.53	3.53	3.54	3.55
Haddon Heights	5.5	3.56	3.58	3.58	3.57	3.58	3.57	3.57	3.57	3.56	3.56	3.56	3.57	3.59	3.58	3.58	3.58	3.58	3.58	3.57	3.56	3.57	3.56	3.56	3.56	3.57	3.56	3.57
Magnolia	7.9	3.58	4.00	4.00	4.00	4.00	3.59	3.59	3.59	3.59	3.58	3.59	4.01	4.01	4.00	4.00	4.00	4.00	4.00	3.59	3.59	3.59	3.59	3.58	3.58	3.59	3.59	3.59
Clementon	12.0	4.02	4.03	4.03	4.03	4.04	4.02	4.02	4.02	4.02	4.01	4.03	4.04	4.01	4.03	4.03	4.03	4.03	4.03	4.02	4.02	4.02	4.02	4.01	4.01	4.02	4.02	4.03
Williamstown J'ct	17.0	4.06	4.07	4.06	4.07	4.08	4.07	4.06	4.06	4.06	4.06	4.07	4.04	4.08	4.07	4.07	4.07	4.07	4.07	4.06	4.06	4.06	4.06	4.05	4.06	4.06	4.06	4.07
Cedar Brook	19.9	4.09	4.10	4.10	4.10	4.10	4.09	4.09	4.09	4.09	4.09	4.09	4.09	4.10	4.09	4.09	4.09	4.09	4.10	4.09	4.09	4.09	4.09	4.08	4.08	4.09	4.09	4.07
Winslow Junc	24.5	4.12	4.13	4.14	4.14	4.13	4.13	4.13	4.12	4.13	4.12	4.12	4.11	4.11	4.13	4.14	4.14	4.14	4.14	4.13	4.12	4.12	4.12	4.12	4.12	4.12	4.12	4.12
Hammonton	27.6	4.15	4.16	4.16	4.16	4.16	4.15	4.15	4.15	4.15	4.14	4.14	4.15	4.14	4.15	4.17	4.16	4.16	4.16	4.16	4.15	4.15	4.15	4.15	4.14	4.15	4.15	4.15
Elwood	33.8	4.20	4.20	4.21	4.20	4.21	4.20	4.20	4.20	4.20	4.19	4.19	4.20	4.21	4.22	4.20	4.20	4.24	4.20	4.19	4.23	4.19	4.20	4.24	4.19	4.19	4.19	4.20
Egg Harbor	38.7	4.24	4.25	4.25	4.24	4.25	4.24	4.24	4.24	4.24	4.24	4.24	4.23	4.24	4.26	4.24	4.24	4.24	4.24	4.25	4.23	4.24	4.24	4.24	4.23	4.23	4.23	4.23
Brigantine Junc	43.5	4.28	4.28	4.29	4.29	4.29	4.28	4.28	4.28	4.28	4.27	4.27	4.28	4.28	4.29	4.28	4.27	4.28	4.28	4.29	4.27	4.27	4.27	4.27	4.26	4.26	4.26	4.27
Pleasantville	50.5	4.33	4.34	4.35	4.34	4.35	4.33	4.33	4.33	4.33	4.33	4.33	4.32	4.34	4.35	4.32	4.33	4.32	4.33	4.34	4.32	4.33	4.32	4.33	4.32	4.32	4.32	4.33
Meadow Tower	53.8	4.37	4.37	4.37	4.37	4.37	4.35	4.36	4.36	4.36	4.35	4.34	4.36	4.36	4.37	4.35	4.34	4.36	4.36	4.37	4.35	4.36	4.35	4.36	4.35	4.35	4.35	4.35
Atlantic City	55.5	4.40	4.38	4.38	4.38	4.38	4.37	4.37	4.37	4.37	4.36	4.36	4.38	4.38	4.39	4.38	4.38	4.38	4.38	4.38	4.38	4.38	4.39	4.38	4.38	4.37	4.37	4.38
Number of Cars			5	5	5	5	5	5	5	5	5	5	5	5	5	5	5	5	5	5	6	6	5	5	5	6	6	6
Passengers carried			196	260	138	128	154	206	307	150	116	25	171	184	314	150	146	192	195	253	376	157	127	123	161	204	386
Running Time			48	47	47	47	47	48	48	48	48		47	47	47	47	47	47	47	48	47	50		49	48	48	47
Miles per hr. (ave)			69.3	69.7	70.1	70.1	70.8	69.3	69.3	69.0	69.3	71.6	68.3	70.8	69.3	70.8	70.8	70.8	70.1	68.6	67.9	66.6	67.9	67.6	67.9	69.3	70.3

AUGUST

Stations	Distance	Schd. Time	2d	3d	4th	6th	7th	9th	10th	11th	12th	13th	14th	16th	17th	18th	19th	20th	21st	23d	24th	26th	27th	28th	29th	30th	31st
Camden	.0	3.48	3.51	3.51	3.51	3.50	3.49	3.50	3.50	3.49	3.50	3.50	3.51	3.51	3.51	3.51	3.51	3.51	3.51	3.49	3.49	3.49	3.49	3.49	3.49	3.50	3.51
West Collingswood	3.1	3.54	3.56	3.56	3.56	3.55	3.54	3.55	3.55	3.54	3.55	3.55	3.56	3.56	3.56	3.56	3.55	3.55	3.56	3.54	3.54	3.54	3.55	3.54	3.54	3.55	3.55
Haddon Heights	5.5	3.56	3.59	3.59	3.59	3.58	3.56	3.57	3.58	3.57	3.57	3.57	3.58	3.59	3.58	3.58	3.58	3.58	3.57	3.56	3.57	3.56	3.57	3.57	3.57	3.57	3.58
Magnolia	7.9	3.58	4.01	4.01	4.01	4.00	3.59	3.59	4.00	3.59	3.59	3.59	4.01	4.00	4.00	4.00	4.00	4.00	4.01	3.59	3.59	3.59	4.00	3.59	3.59	4.00	4.00
Clementon	12.0	4.02	4.04	4.04	4.04	4.03	4.02	4.02	4.03	4.02	4.02	4.03	4.04	4.04	4.03	4.03	4.04	4.03	4.04	4.02	4.02	4.02	4.03	4.02	4.02	4.02	4.03
Williamstown J'ct	17.0	4.06	4.08	4.06	4.07	4.07	4.06	4.06	4.07	4.07	4.06	4.07	4.08	4.08	4.08	4.08	4.08	4.07	4.09	4.06	4.06	4.06	4.07	4.06	4.06	4.06	4.07
Cedar Brook	19.9	4.09	4.11	4.11	4.11	4.10	4.09	4.09	4.09	4.09	4.09	4.10	4.11	4.11	4.08	4.08	4.10	4.09	4.12	4.09	4.09	4.09	4.09	4.09	4.09	4.09	4.10
Winslow Junc	24.5	4.12	4.14	4.15	4.14	4.13	4.12	4.12	4.14	4.12	4.12	4.13	4.14	4.11	4.11	4.13	4.14	4.13	4.12	4.13	4.12	4.12	4.13	4.12	4.12	4.09	4.13
Hammonton	27.6	4.15	4.17	4.17	4.17	4.16	4.15	4.15	4.16	4.15	4.15	4.15	4.17	4.14	4.14	4.13	4.14	4.14	4.16	4.15	4.14	4.14	4.15	4.14	4.12	4.12	4.13
Elwood	33.8	4.20	4.21	4.21	4.21	4.20	4.20	4.20	4.21	4.19	4.20	4.20	4.21	4.21	4.20	4.20	4.21	4.20	4.17	4.19	4.19	4.19	4.20	4.19	4.15	4.15	4.15
Egg Harbor	38.7	4.24	4.25	4.25	4.24	4.24	4.24	4.23	4.23	4.23	4.24	4.25	4.25	4.25	4.24	4.24	4.25	4.24	4.22	4.23	4.23	4.23	4.24	4.23	4.23	4.23	4.20
Brigantine Junc	43.5	4.28	4.29	4.29	4.29	4.28	4.27	4.27	4.28	4.27	4.27	4.27	4.29	4.29	4.28	4.28	4.28	4.27	4.26	4.27	4.27	4.27	4.27	4.27	4.23	4.23	4.24
Pleasantville	50.5	4.33	4.34	4.34	4.34	4.33	4.33	4.33	4.34	4.32	4.33	4.33	4.35	4.34	4.34	4.34	4.34	4.34	4.35	4.32	4.32	4.32	4.33	4.33	4.31	4.32	4.33
Meadow Tower	53.8	4.36	4.37	4.37	4.37	4.36	4.35	4.35	4.37	4.35	4.35	4.35	4.37	4.37	4.36	4.36	4.36	4.36	4.38	4.35	4.35	4.35	4.36	4.36	4.34	4.35	4.36
Atlantic City	55.5	4.40	4.38	4.39	4.39	4.38	4.37	4.38	4.38	4.37	4.36	4.37	4.39	4.39	4.38	4.38	4.38	4.37	4.40	4.38	4.38	4.38	4.38	4.37	4.35	4.38	4.37
Number of Cars			6	6	6	6	6	5	5	6	6	6	6	6	6	6	5	5	6	5	6	5	5	5	6	5	5
Passengers carried			252	238	265	185	383	223	262	257	283	292	448	267	292	236	232	276	396	178	190	211	195	259	370	147	166
Running Time			46	47	48	48	48	47	48	48	48	47	48	47	46	47	47	46	48	48	48	49	49	48	48	47	46
Miles per hr. (ave)			71.2	70.1	69.3	69.3	69.3	69.7	69.3	69.3	69.3	70.1	69.3	69.7	71.2	70.1	70.8	71.2	69.0	68.6	68.6	67.9	67.9	68.3	69.0	69.7	71.2

In March, 1899, two locomotives were built for the Chicago, Burlington and Quincy Railroad, for the fast mail service west of Chicago. These were of the Atlantic type with Vauclain compound cylinders, thirteen and one-half and twenty-three inches in diameter, and twenty-six inches stroke; driving wheels eighty-four and one-quarter inches in diameter; weight, in working

ATLANTIC TYPE LOCOMOTIVE
For Chicago, Burlington and Quincy Railroad

order, eighty-five thousand eight hundred and fifty pounds on driving wheels, and one hundred and fifty-nine thousand pounds total of engine. The total weight of engine and tender complete was about two hundred and fifty-four thousand pounds. An illustration of one of these locomotives is shown above.

Dr. Edward H. Williams, who had been connected with the Works as a partner since 1870, died December 21, 1899, at Santa Barbara, California.

The year 1899 was marked by a large increase in foreign business, notably in England and France. Contracts were made in England covering thirty locomotives for the Midland Railway, twenty locomotives for the Great Northern Railway, and twenty locomotives for the Great Central Railway. Ten locomotives were also ordered by the French State Railways, and ten by the Bone Guelma Railway, in the French colonies of Algiers.

COMPOUND ATLANTIC TYPE LOCOMOTIVE
For the Bavarian State Railways

In the fall of this year two Vauclain compound Consolidation freight locomotives were built for the Bavarian State Railways. These were ordered as samples, the company practically announcing its intention of modeling future locomotives for their freight traffic after these engines. So well did these sample locomotives perform, that in the following year, the management decided to order two passenger engines of the compound Atlantic type, and also embody in their passenger motive power the new features contained in these machines.

The Baldwin Locomotive Works exhibited two locomotives at the Paris Exposition of 1900—a "goods" locomotive of the Mogul type for the Great Northern Railway, of England, and an Atlantic type passenger locomotive for the French State Railways. The exhibit of the French State Railways also included a compound American type passenger locomotive built by the Baldwin Locomotive Works. These engines were built in the regular course of business for the companies whose names they bore, and went into service on these roads immediately after the Exposition was over. In this year also large orders were filled for the Chinese Eastern Railroad, the Paris-Orleans Railway, the Finland State, the Egyptian State and the Belgian State Railways.

The beginning of the twentieth century witnessed great industrial prosperity in America and large demands for railway freight transportation. The introduction of cars of large capacity became general on American railroads, a tendency

COMPOUND PRAIRIE TYPE LOCOMOTIVE
For the Atchison, Topeka and Santa Fe Railway

which had been gradually developing for some years. This involved increased train tonnage, improved road beds, heavier rails, stronger bridges and more powerful locomotives. The

locomotive has always reflected the changes in railroad practice. Just as the demand for increased horse power, involving
greater steaming capacity and a larger grate area, evolved the
Atlantic type engine from the American or eight-wheeled passenger engine; so, in order to secure a locomotive with ample
heating surface and suitable firebox to handle heavy trains at
high speed, the Prairie type was designed, being a logical development of the Mogul and Ten-wheeled engines. The Prairie type
engine has a leading pony truck, three pairs of driving wheels,
and a wide firebox extending over the frames and placed back of
the driving wheels. To support this overhanging weight, a pair
of trailing wheels is placed underneath the firebox. Fifty locomotives of this type were built for the Chicago, Burlington and
Quincy Railroad, and forty-five for the Atchison, Topeka and
Santa Fe Railway, in 1901.

At the Pan-American Exposition, held at Buffalo, N. Y.,
during 1901, a new departure in locomotive practice was exhibited by the Baldwin Locomotive Works. This was a Ten-
wheeled locomotive, built for the Illinois Central Railroad,
the firebox and tender of which were of special construction,
embodying the inventions of Mr. Cornelius Vanderbilt, M.E.
The firebox was cylindrical in form, with annular corrugations,

TEN-WHEELED LOCOMOTIVE
With Vanderbilt Boiler and Tender

its axis eccentric to that of the boiler. It was riveted to the back
head of the boiler, and was supported at the bottom by the mud
rings; but otherwise was entirely disconnected from the outer
shell, thus eliminating stay bolts and crown bars, necessary to
flat surfaces in usual construction. It was supposed that the
ease with which the firebox could be removed, and the absence
of the usual repairs incidental to the renewal of stay bolts, would

commend it. Defects developed, however, which caused this type of boiler to be abandoned after a few years' trial. The feature of the tender was a cylindrical instead of the ordinary U-shaped tank placed back of the coal space, the advantage being a better distribution of weight, and a smaller proportion of dead weight to carrying capacity. These tenders are still being built when specified by railroad companies.

The year 1901 was especially noticeable for the large volume of domestic business handled, there being great demand for motive power from the railroads of the West and Southwest. Large orders were placed with the Baldwin Locomotive Works in this year by the Union Pacific; Chicago, Burlington and Quincy; Choctaw, Oklahoma and Gulf; Toledo, St. Louis and Western; Atchison, Topeka and Santa Fe; Chicago and Alton; Missouri, Kansas and Texas; Chicago, Milwaukee and St. Paul, and Southern Pacific Railroads. The Pennsylvania Railroad in this year, ordered over one hundred and fifty locomotives of various types from the Baldwin Locomotive Works, and the Baltimore and Ohio Railroad also placed an order for over one hundred locomotives.

The locomotives built for export, during 1901, included ten for the New Zealand Government Railways, which were designed to use lignite as fuel. They had three pairs of coupled driving-wheels, a four-wheeled leading truck, and a two-wheeled trailing truck, over which was placed a deep, wide firebox. This type subsequently became known as the "Pacific," and because of its high steaming capacity and adhesion, was built in large numbers for heavy passenger service in the United States.

The month of February, 1902, witnessed the completion of the twenty thousandth locomotive built by the Baldwin Locomotive Works. This engine embodied several interesting features, including a new arrangement of Vauclain compound cylinders. In the compound locomotives previously constructed, a high and a low pressure cylinder had been used on each side of the locomotive, the two cylinders on the same side being placed one above the other. In locomotive No. 20,000 the axes of the four cylinders were placed in the same horizontal plane, the two high pressure cylinders being between the frames and the two low pressure outside. The high pressure pistons were connected to cranks, placed on the axle of the first pair of driving wheels; while the low pressure pistons were connected to crank pins outside the

BALANCED COMPOUND LOCOMOTIVE
Baldwin Engine No. 20,000

wheels, in the usual manner. With this construction there were of course four sets of guides, as well as four crossheads and main rods. The two cranks on the axle were placed ninety degrees apart, and each of them was one hundred and eighty degrees from the corresponding crank pin on the outside of the wheel. The two pistons on the same side of the locomotive thus opposed one another in movement, starting their strokes simultaneously

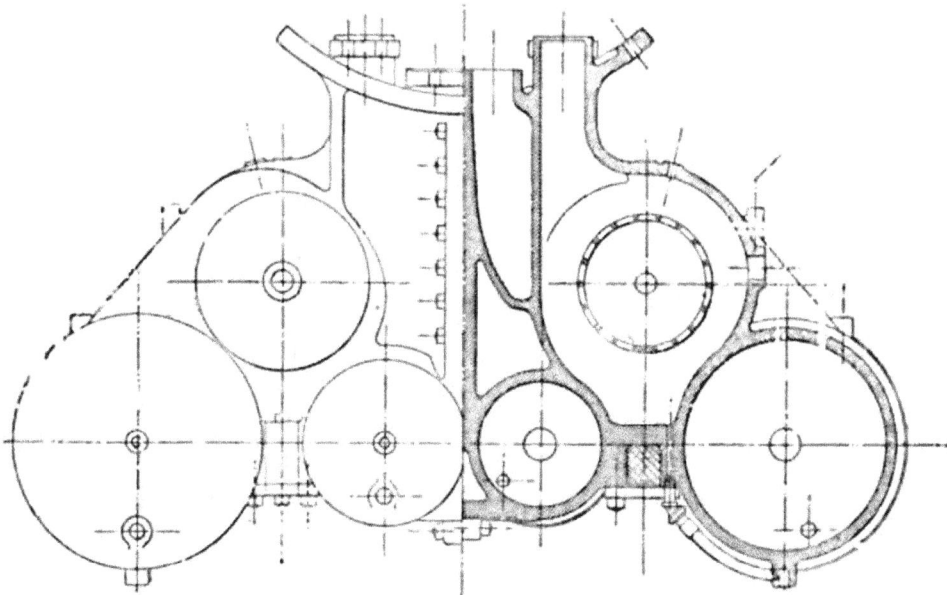

CROSS SECTION OF BALANCED COMPOUND CYLINDERS

from opposite ends of their respective cylinders. With this construction, the disturbing effects of the reciprocating weights are partially neutralized; and no excess weight need be used in counterbalancing the driving wheels. This obviates the so-called "hammer blow," which is always present in locomotives having outside cylinders only. Balanced compound locomotives, as described above, can carry a maximum load on driving wheels without detriment to the track, as the greatest pressure on the rail is that due to the static wheel load.

In balanced compound locomotives of the Vauclain type, the steam distribution to each pair of cylinders is controlled by a single piston valve, so that the valve gear is no more complicated than that of a single expansion locomotive. Upward of five hundred of these locomotives had been built up to the close of 1912, the majority of them for fast passenger service. With the advent of high temperature superheating, however, the building of this type of locomotive for American railroads practically ceased.

The construction of the twenty thousandth locomotive and the completion of seventy years of continuous operation were celebrated on the evening of February 27, 1902, at the Union League, of Philadelphia, by a banquet at which two hundred and fifty guests, including many of the most representative men in the United States, were present.

In May, 1902, a Decapod locomotive was built for the Atchison, Topeka and Santa Fe Railway. This was the first tandem compound in the experience of the Works and the heaviest locomotive built up to that time. The total weight of the engine alone was two hundred and sixty-seven thousand eight hundred pounds, of which two hundred and thirty-seven thousand eight hundred pounds were on the five pairs of driving wheels. It was designed for heavy freight hauling on the steep grades encountered on one section of this road.

The first locomotive built in the United States to burn lignite fuel was constructed in this year for the Bismarck, Washburn and Great Falls Railway. The Mikado type was selected in order to secure sufficient grate area and firebox volume. The design is illustrated on page 95. Mikado type locomotives were subsequently built in large numbers for heavy freight service in the United States.

MIKADO TYPE LOCOMOTIVE
For the Bismarck, Washburn and Great Falls Railway

The discovery of large quantities of crude petroleum in gushers located in the Beaumont oil fields, of Texas, caused the railroads tapping this field to adopt, to some extent, this fuel on their locomotives. Oil-burning locomotives were built for the Atchison, Topeka and Santa Fe, the Southern Pacific, and the Galveston, Houston and Henderson Railroads, in 1902. Since that date, oil has practically replaced coal as a locomotive fuel in the Southwest. Oil-burning locomotives have also been introduced in the Pacific Coast District and the far Northwest.

With the increased use of electrically driven trains for interurban, elevated and subway traffic, many orders were received for electric motor trucks in this year. Electrical locomotives, both for surface and mine haulage, showed a marked increase in this year also, both in variety of design and the number constructed.

In the year 1903 the Baldwin Locomotive Works completed two thousand and twenty-two locomotives, its largest annual

TANDEM COMPOUND SANTA FE TYPE LOCOMOTIVE
For the Atchison, Topeka and Santa Fe Railway

output up to that time. Among these were four four-cylinder

balanced compound Atlantic type locomotives for the Atchison, Topeka and Santa Fe Railway, which proved highly successful. The same road received twenty-six single-expansion Pacific type locomotives for heavy passenger service, and also a consignment of tandem compound locomotives for freight service. These engines were similar to the Decapod locomotive previously described, except that a trailing truck was added. This improved the curving qualities of the engines when running backward. To this type the name Santa Fe was given.

During the year 1903, standard locomotive designs were prepared at these Works for the Associated Lines, which at that time comprised the Southern Pacific Company, Union Pacific Railroad, Oregon Short Line Railroad, Oregon Railroad and Navigation Company, and the Chicago and Alton Railway. As the various lines were already equipped with sufficient light power, only heavy designs for common standards were adopted. Six such designs were prepared: an Atlantic and a Pacific type locomotive for passenger service, two sizes of Consolidation engines for freight service, a Mogul locomotive for fast freight, and a six-wheeled switcher.

Owing to the rapid increase in the production of the Works, additional erecting facilities were required; and in 1903 a new erecting shop, arranged on a novel plan, was completed at Twenty-sixth Street and Pennsylvania Avenue. This shop was built in the form of a round house, having twenty-seven stalls, with an eighty foot turntable in the center. It was used principally for finishing and testing purposes.

In 1904 there was a temporary falling off in production, one thousand four hundred and eighty-five locomotives being completed during that year. At the Louisiana Purchase Exposition, held at St. Louis, from May to November of this year, the Baldwin Locomotive Works exhibited the following locomotives:

STANDARD GAUGE.—A balanced compound Atlantic type locomotive, for the Atchison, Topeka and Santa Fe Railway. (Illustrated on page 97). A four-cylinder compound Atlantic type locomotive for the Chicago, Burlington and Quincy Railroad. (This engine had been built two years previously, and was withdrawn from service to be placed on exhibition). A tandem compound Santa Fe type locomotive for the Atchison, Topeka and Santa Fe Railway. An Atlantic type locomotive for the Chicago and Alton Railway. A Pacific type locomotive

BALANCED COMPOUND ATLANTIC TYPE LOCOMOTIVE
For the Atchison, Topeka and Santa Fe Railway

for the Union Pacific Railroad. A Consolidation type locomotive for the Southern Pacific Company. A Pacific type locomotive for the St. Louis and San Francisco Railroad. A two-cylinder compound Consolidation type locomotive for the Norfolk and Western Railway. A single-expansion Consolidation type locomotive for the Norfolk and Western Railway. A ten-wheeled locomotive for the Norfolk and Western Railway. An Atlantic type locomotive for the Norfolk and Western Railway. A Consolidation type locomotive with Wootten firebox, for the Delaware, Lackawanna and Western Railroad. A Mogul type locomotive for the Missouri, Kansas and Texas Railway.

There were also shown four examples of electric trucks, which were designed for standard gauge track.

NARROW GAUGE.—An electric mining locomotive for the Norfolk Coal and Coke Company. (Gauge three feet six inches). An electric mining locomotive for the Berwind-White Coal Mining Company. (Gauge three feet). An electric locomotive for industrial haulage. (Gauge two feet). The electric locomotives and trucks were exhibited in the Palace of Electricity in conjunction with the Westinghouse Electric and Manufacturing Company, which furnished the electrical equipment.

During this year three Mallet compound articulated locomotives, designed for meter gauge, were built for the American Railroad of Porto Rico. One of these engines is illustrated on page 98. These locomotives had three pairs of driving wheels, thirty-seven inches in diameter, in each group The total weight was one hundred and six thousand six hundred and fifty pounds, and the tractive force twenty thousand two

MALLET ARTICULATED COMPOUND LOCOMOTIVE
For the American Railroad of Porto Rico

hundred pounds working compound. These were the first Mallet articulated locomotives built in the experience of the Works.

Among other interesting locomotives exported during 1904, may be mentioned sixteen tank engines for the Imperial Government Railways of Japan. These locomotives had three pairs of driving wheels and a two-wheeled rear truck. They were con-

SIX COUPLED TANK LOCOMOTIVE
For the Imperial Government Railways of Japan

structed with plate frames, in accordance with specifications furnished by the railway company. One hundred and fifty additional locomotives of the same type were built during the following year.

Toward the close of the year 1904 the output began to increase, and in 1905, two thousand two hundred and fifty locomotives were turned out. Among these were five hundred and seventy-two engines for the Pennsylvania Railroad System, including the lines east and west of Pittsburg. One hundred and sixty of these locomotives, all of the Consolidation type, were completed between October 10th and November 22d. This year witnessed the introduction of the Walschaerts valve motion on several American railroads. It was applied to a large number of the Pennsylvania Railroad engines above referred to, and also to thirty-eight ten-wheeled locomotives for the Chicago, Rock Island and Pacific Railway.

Among the locomotives exported during the year 1905, may be mentioned twenty of the ten-wheeled type, built for the New South Wales Government Railways. These engines were built to the railway company's drawings and specifications. A large number of special features, including plate frames and the Allen valve motion, entered into their construction.

During the year 1906 a number of large electric locomotives were furnished to the New York, New Haven and Hartford Railroad Company, for the purpose of replacing steam locomotives in the vicinity of New York City. Each of these locomotives was mounted on two four-wheeled trucks, and equipped with four single phase alternating current motors, which rotated the axles without intermediate gearing. The nominal capacity of each unit was one thousand horsepower.

In 1906, the Great Northern Railway received five Mallet articulated locomotives, which were the heaviest, at that time,

MALLET COMPOUND ARTICULATED LOCOMOTIVE
For the Great Northern Railway

in the experience of the Works. These locomotives were carried on six pairs of driving wheels divided into two groups, and a two-wheeled truck front and back. They weighed three hundred and fifty-five thousand pounds, of which three hundred and sixteen thousand pounds were carried on the driving wheels. One of these locomotives is illustrated on the previous page.

During this year an order was also received for fifty-seven balanced compound Prairie type locomotives for the Atchison, Topeka and Santa Fe Railway. These locomotives were designed for fast freight service, and had inside high-pressure

BALANCED COMPOUND PRAIRIE TYPE LOCOMOTIVE
For the Atchison, Topeka and Santa Fe Railway

cylinders, inclined at an angle of seven degrees, in order that their main rods could clear the first driving axle. The total weight in working order was two hundred and forty-eight thousand two hundred pounds, of which the driving wheels carry one hundred and seventy-four thousand seven hundred pounds. One of them is illustrated above. Thirty-one similar locomotives were built in 1907.

Among the important foreign orders filled during the year 1906, may be mentioned one from the Italian Government Rail-

BALANCED COMPOUND TEN-WHEELED LOCOMOTIVE
For the Italian Government Railways

ways for twenty locomotives. The number was equally divided between balanced compound ten-wheeled locomotives for passenger service, and single-expansion Consolidation locomotives for freight service. One of the passenger locomotives is illustrated on the previous page.

Owing to the increasing demand for electric trucks, a new shop equipped with the most approved machinery for turning out this class of work, was built early in 1906. This shop had a capacity of one hundred trucks per week.

During the same year, a tract of one hundred and eighty-four acres was purchased at Eddystone, Pa., about twelve miles from the city, where extensive foundries and blacksmith shops were erected. The removal of these shops from the Philadelphia plant, allowed room for additional machine and erecting shops.

A life size bronze statue of Matthias W. Baldwin was unveiled on June 2, 1906, and presented by the Baldwin Locomotive Works to the Park Commission of the City of Philadelphia. This statue occupies a prominent position in front of the main office.

On December 31, 1906, Mr. George Burnham, Jr., who had been a member of the firm since 1896, retired from the partnership.

On January 29, 1907, fire partially destroyed the shop building located at the southeast corner of Fifteenth and Spring Garden Streets. The several departments affected were at once moved into other quarters, and work was continued with but little delay.

SANTA FE TYPE LOCOMOTIVE
For the Pittsburg, Shawmut and Northern Railroad

In February, 1907, the thirty-thousandth locomotive was completed. This engine was of the Santa Fe type, having single-expansion cylinders and a smokebox superheater. It was built for the Pittsburg, Shawmut and Northern Railroad Company, and is illustrated on the previous page.

In May and June, 1907, twenty balanced compound locomotives of the ten-wheeled type were completed for the Paris-Orleans Railway of France. The compound features were arranged on the deGlehn system, and the engines were built throughout to drawings and specifications furnished by the railway company. All measurements were made on the metric system, this being the first instance in the experience of the Works where metric standards were used exclusively in the con-

BALANCED COMPOUND LOCOMOTIVE
For the Paris-Orleans Railway of France

struction of a locomotive. An illustration of one of these engines is presented herewith.

At the Jamestown Ter-Centennial Exposition, held at Norfolk, Va., in 1907, the Works exhibited five steam locomotives, three Baldwin-Westinghouse electric locomotives, and three electric trucks.

During this same year (1907), twenty Consolidation type locomotives and two inspection cars were built for the South Manchurian Railways. All these locomotives were of standard gauge.

The financial depression, which began during the fall of 1907, resulted in a greatly decreased demand for railway supplies of all kinds, and the year 1908 witnessed the completion of only six hundred and seventeen locomotives, of which one hundred and seventy-four were exported. Among the latter may be mentioned a Mallet articulated compound locomotive of the 2-6-6-2 type, which was built for plantation service in San Domingo. This locomotive developed a tractive force of ten thousand five hundred pounds, which was remarkable in consideration of the fact that it was of only two feet six inches gauge, and was suitable for use on twenty-five pound rails.

Mr. William P. Henszey, who had been identified with the Works since March 7, 1859, and a member of the firm since 1870, died on March 23, 1909. Mr. Henszey had had an unusually

WILLIAM P. HENSZEY

wide experience in all branches of locomotive engineering, and even after his retirement as Chief Mechanical Engineer, he spent much time in the draughting room at the Works, and his advice was constantly sought. He was largely responsible for the standardization of locomotive details and for the perfecting of a system of manufacture, whereby like parts of engines of the same class were made interchangeable. Many successful locomotives of unusual types, which were built to meet difficult service requirements, were the direct result of his ingenuity and skill as a designer.

At the Alaska-Yukon-Pacific Exposition held at Seattle, Washington, in 1909, two locomotives were exhibited: a Mallet articulated compound for the Great Northern Railway, and a balanced compound Atlantic type for the Spokane, Portland and Seattle Railway.

During this year, an important change in organization was effected. On July 1, 1909, the partnership of Burnham, Williams & Co. was dissolved, and a stock company under the name of

JOHN H. CONVERSE

Baldwin Locomotive Works was incorporated under the laws of the State of Pennsylvania with the following officers:

John H. Converse, President
Alba B. Johnson, Vice-President and Treasurer
William L. Austin, Vice-President and Engineer
Samuel M. Vauclain, General Superintendent
William deKrafft, Secretary and Assistant Treasurer

The above officers constituted the Board of Directors.

The great growth of the business and its need for a larger working capital, led to the issue on April 1, 1910, of ten million dollars first mortgage five per cent. bonds.

John H. Converse, who had been connected with the Works since 1870 and a partner since 1873, died at his home in Philadelphia on May 3, 1910. Throughout the forty years of his connection with the Works, whilst Mr. Converse was occupied primarily with the general financial and commercial administration of the business, he was also deeply interested in every improvement in locomotive engineering. He took an active part in civic, philanthropic and religious interests. He was succeeded as President of the Company by William L. Austin.

On July 1, 1911, the entire property owned by Baldwin Locomotive Works was sold to a new corporation known as the Philadelphia Locomotive Works. This was immediately reorganized as The Baldwin Locomotive Works. This is a public joint stock company, organized under the laws of Pennsylvania, and capitalized subject to the mortgage bonds above mentioned at $40,000,000 ($20,000,000 cumulative preferred stock and $20,000,000 common stock). The stock is listed on the Philadelphia and New York Exchanges.

The first Board of Directors of the new company was composed as follows:

William L. Austin, Chairman; Roland L. Taylor, Alba B. Johnson, Samuel MacRoberts, Samuel M. Vauclain, Charles D. Norton, Edward T. Stotesbury, Otis H. Cutler, Edmund C. Converse, Francis M. Weld, T. deWitt Cuyler, William Burnham.

The officers of the new company were as follows:

William L. Austin, Chairman of the Board
Alba B. Johnson, President
Samuel M. Vauclain, Vice President
William deKrafft, Secretary and Treasurer

In 1910, the first Baldwin internal combustion locomotives, built in accordance with patents granted to A. H. Ehle, were constructed; and thereafter these machines assumed a permanent place among the products of the Works. These locomotives are distinctive, principally in that they employ no chains whatever; the final drive being through specially designed side-rods. This allows freedom of the driving-wheels and spring suspension of all the principal parts, including the motor, frames and transmission. There are no sliding gears in the transmission, the

different gear ratios being obtained by the engagement of positive
jaw clutches; while the gears remain constantly in mesh. These
locomotives are specially suitable for industrial, contractors'
and light switching service. They were first built in four standard
sizes, weighing respectively three and one-half, five, seven and
nine tons. Subsequently a larger size, weighing twenty-three
tons, and suitable for standard gauge only, was added. In 1919,
the designs were revised to include five sizes, weighing from five
to twenty-five tons.

An illustration of a Baldwin internal combustion locomotive
is presented on page 120.

In 1911, the Board of Directors authorized the purchase of a
tract of three hundred and seventy acres at East Chicago, Indiana.
Plans were subsequently developed for the construction of works
for the manufacture of tires and wheels, as part of the business
of the Standard Steel Works Co., and for the building of locomotives, as part of the business of The Baldwin Locomotive Works.
Up to 1919, however, these shops had not been constructed.

The subject of superheating was receiving much attention
at this time, and a large number of superheaters were applied
to locomotives built during 1911 and 1912. In the majority

BALANCED COMPOUND PACIFIC TYPE LOCOMOTIVE
For the Atchison, Topeka and Santa Fe Railway

of cases superheaters of the fire-tube type were used, in accordance
with patents controlled by the Locomotive Superheater Co.
The Vauclain type of smokebox superheater, originally designed
in 1905, was also used to some extent, but service tests firmly
established the economies due to high superheat, and the use of
the fire-tube superheater, on large locomotives, is now practically

universal. Superheaters in conjunction with compound cylinders are employed on Mallet locomotives; and they have also been used, to a limited extent, on balanced compound locomotives built for the Atchison, Topeka & Santa Fe Ry. An illustration of a Pacific type locomotive, so equipped, is shown on the previous page.

The successful introduction of the superheater in American locomotive practice, was followed by the construction of locomotives for all classes of service, of materially greater capacity than those previously built. This increase in capacity was accompanied by the extensive use of such labor-saving devices as mechanical stokers, coal pushers on tenders, and power operated fire-doors and grate shakers. In fact, without the use of these devices it would be difficult to operate, at full capacity, the largest locomotives now in service.

Reference has been made to a design of heavy freight locomotive known as the Mikado, which has four pairs of coupled driving-wheels with a two-wheeled leading and two-wheeled trailing truck. Since 1909, this type has come into extensive use on American railroads, and, because of its increased steaming capacity, has largely replaced the Consolidation type for main-

SANTA FE TYPE LOCOMOTIVE
For the Chicago, Burlington and Quincy Railroad

line service. A development of the Mikado type is found in the Santa Fe, with five pairs of coupled driving-wheels. Locomotives of the Santa Fe type, as has been mentioned, were built for the Atchison, Topeka & Santa Fe Ry. in 1903; but it was about ten years later before this type began to be used, to any considerable extent, on other roads. In the spring of 1912, the Chicago, Burlington & Quincy R. R. placed in service five locomotives of the Santa Fe type, one of which is illustrated on page 107. These locomotives had cylinders thirty inches in diameter by thirty-two inches stroke, and driving-wheels sixty inches in diameter. They weighed, in working order, three hundred and seventy-eight thousand seven hundred pounds, of which three hundred and one thousand eight hundred pounds were carried on the driving-wheels. These locomotives were followed by a large number of others of similar type, which were built not only for the Burlington System, but also for various other roads throughout the country.

In 1910, a Mikado type locomotive, designed to burn lignite fuel, was built for the Oregon Railroad and Navigation Company. This locomotive was constructed in accordance with specifications prepared by Mr. J. F. Graham, Superintendent of Motive Power, and the design was based on that of the standard Consolidation type locomotives for the Associated Lines. The new Mikado had cylinders twenty-three and three-quarters inches in diameter by thirty inches stroke, and driving-wheels fifty-seven inches in diameter; and it weighed in working order, exclusive of tender, two-hundred and sixty-three thousand pounds. This locomotive proved highly successful, and the Mikado type locomotives subsequently built for the Union and Southern Pacific Systems and their associated lines, were directly based upon it.

LIGNITE-BURNING MIKADO TYPE LOCOMOTIVE
For the Oregon Railroad and Navigation Co.

A large number of Mallet locomotives were built during this period, for pushing and heavy road service on steep grades. Among the most interesting of these were two groups of locomotives, one of the 2-8-8-2 type and the other of the 2-6-6-2 type, constructed for the Southern Pacific Co. and used in freight and passenger service respectively.   In order to give the engine-men a better view when running through tunnels and snow-sheds, these locomotives were operated with the cab end leading, the

MALLET ARTICULATED FREIGHT LOCOMOTIVE
For the Southern Pacific Co.

tender being coupled to the smoke-box end.   As oil was used for fuel, this arrangement was entirely practicable.   An illus-tration of one of the freight locomotives is presented herewith.

In the years 1910 and 1911, six locomotives of the 2-6-6-2 type, which were included in a large number built for the Atchi-son, Topeka & Santa Fe Ry., were fitted with articulated boilers. The front boiler section, instead of being supported on sliding bearings, was rigidly mounted on the frames, and was attached

ARTICULATED LOCOMOTIVE WITH FLEXIBLE BOILER
For the Atchison, Topeka and Santa Fe Railway

to the rear boiler section by a flexible connection.   The illustra-tion shows one of these locomotives, in which the flexible con-nection consisted of a series of rings, fastened together to form a bellows-shaped structure.   This arrangement was built in accordance with patents granted to Samuel M. Vauclain.

An interesting group of eighteen Mallet locomotives was completed in 1912 for the Imperial Government Rys. of Japan. These locomotives were of the 0-6-6-0 type, and had a gauge of three feet six inches. They were equipped with superheaters.

MALLET ARTICULATED LOCOMOTIVE
For the Imperial Government Railways of Japan

and weighed, exclusive of tenders, one hundred and forty-two thousand six hundred and fifty pounds each. The accompanying illustration shows the design.

Locomotive number forty thousand was completed in June, 1913. It was of the Pacific (4-6-2) type, and was built for the Pennsylvania Lines West of Pittsburgh, to drawings and specifications furnished by the Railway Company. Since 1903, Pacific type locomotives have been built to a constantly increasing extent, for heavy passenger service; and locomotive

PACIFIC TYPE LOCOMOTIVE
For the Pennsylvania Lines.   Baldwin Locomotive No. 40,000

number forty thousand was, at the time of its construction, among the largest in service. This locomotive had cylinders measuring twenty-six by twenty-six inches, and driving wheels eighty inches in diameter; and it weighed, in working order, three hundred and two thousand pounds. It was equipped with a superheater and was fired by a mechanical stoker of the Crawford under-feed type. An illustration of the locomotive is presented on page 110.

In September, 1913, the Erie Railroad ordered a locomotive of the triple articulated type, which was designed and built in accordance with patents granted to George R. Henderson, who at that time was Consulting Engineer of The Baldwin Locomotive Works. This locomotive has the 2-8-8-8-2 wheel arrangement, and is practically a Mallet, with a steam driven tender. In this way, a tractive force equal to that of three Consolidation or Mikado type locomotives can be developed in a single unit. The triple locomotive has six cylinders, all of which are of the same size and cast from the same pattern. The two cylinders which drive the middle group of wheels receive superheated steam direct from the boiler and thus act as the high pressure cylinders; and they exhaust into the front and rear cylinders, which act as the low pressure. The exhaust from the front cylinders is discharged up the stack to create a draught for the fire, while that from the rear cylinders, after passing through a feed-water heater, escapes up a pipe at the rear of the tank. Pumps are used to force the heated feed-water into the boiler.

The first locomotive of this type was completed in April, 1914, and was placed in pushing service on a heavy grade near Susquehanna, Penna. It was named "Matt H. Shay," after the

TRIPLE ARTICULATED LOCOMOTIVE
For the Erie R. R.

oldest living engineer then in the service of the Erie. The cylinders of this locomotive are thirty-six inches in diameter by thirty-two inches stroke, and the driving-wheels are sixty-three inches in diameter. The total weight of the locomotive in working order is eight hundred and fifty-three thousand pounds, and the maximum tractive force exerted is one hundred and sixty thousand pounds. On a test run to determine its hauling capacity on practically level track, the "Matt H. Shay" has hauled a train of two hundred and fifty loaded cars having a length of one and six-tenths miles and weighing seventeen thousand nine hundred and twelve tons. This load was hauled up a maximum grade of 0.09 per cent., combined with a curve of five degrees.

After this locomotive had been fully tried out, two more of similar dimensions were built for the Erie R. R. and completed in 1916. Another of the same general type was built for the Virginian Railway.

While these developments were taking place in the field of steam locomotive engineering, Baldwin-Westinghouse electric locomotives were becoming increasingly prominent in the product of the Works. Among these locomotives may be mentioned five, which were built in 1910 for service in the Hoosac Tunnel, Mass., on the line of the Boston & Maine R. R. This tunnel is four and three-quarters miles long, and its operation with steam locomotives had become difficult because of the accumulation of smoke and gas, which made it impossible to fully utilize the track capacity of the tunnel. The results

ELECTRIC LOCOMOTIVES
For the New York, New Haven and Hartford Railroad

obtained with electric traction have been most satisfactory, and the capacity of the tunnel has been greatly increased.

Up to the close of 1912, one hundred Baldwin-Westinghouse single-phase locomotives had been built for the New York, New Haven & Hartford R. R. for service on the electrified section of the line between New York and Stamford, Conn. The electrification was subsequently extended to New Haven. The electric locomotives built for this road are of various types, and are used in passenger, freight and switching service. The illustration on page 112 represents ten large New Haven electric locomotives of the articulated type, ready for shipment from The Baldwin Locomotive Works to Pittsburgh, to receive their electrical equipment at the Westinghouse plant.

Another interesting group of electric locomotives were those built for the Norfolk & Western Ry. for service between Bluefield and East Vivian, West Virginia, a distance of thirty miles. This line handles a heavy coal traffic, and its capacity, under steam operation, was limited by the number of trains which could be moved through Elkhorn Tunnel, where the line is single tracked. The tunnel has a length of thirty-one hundred feet, and is approached from the West by a two per cent. grade, and from the East by a grade of two and thirty-six-hundredths per cent. When the road was electrified, twenty steam locomotives of the Mallet type were replaced by twelve electric locomotives, and the capacity of the line was greatly increased because of the higher speed at which the trains could be handled. Each electric locomotive consists of two units having a combined weight of two hundred and seventy tons, each unit being of the 2-4-4-2 type. Two of these locomotives handle a train weighing thirty-two hundred and fifty tons through the tunnel in three minutes; while with steam operation, on account of slow speeds and frequent stalling, it was necessary to allow twenty minutes for three Mallet locomotives to take a train through the tunnel.

The development of electric mine and industrial locomotives, during this period, was characterized by refinement in general design and detailed construction. These Works were pioneers in developing and standardizing plate steel and cast steel bar frames for mine locomotives. The accompanying illustration shows one of these locomotives, equipped with a cast steel frame of the bar type. Greater strength and accessibility were secured with this construction, and also, in many cases, lighter mechanical parts,

ELECTRIC MINING LOCOMOTIVE
With Cast Steel Bar Frames

thus allowing the use of heavier and more powerful electrical equipment for a given total weight of locomotive.

During the past few years a large number of storage battery locomotives have been built for mine and industrial service. The Edison storage battery, because of its light weight and durability, has proved particularly well suited for this kind of work.

The completion at Eddystone, in 1912, of a large erecting shop, provided additional erecting facilities much needed to relieve congestion at the Philadelphia plant. This shop was specially designed for the construction of locomotives of the largest size; it covers over seven and one-half acres of ground,

EDDYSTONE ERECTING SHOP

and has over-all dimensions of four hundred and eighty by eight hundred and eighty feet. The building has a steel frame-work, with concrete foundations and side walls of hollow tile. The roof is laid with reinforced cement tile and the floor is of wooden blocks laid on concrete. An illustration of this shop is presented on the preceding page.

George Burnham, Sr., who entered the Works in 1836, died at his home in West Philadelphia on December 10, 1912, in the ninety-sixth year of his age. Mr. Burnham had been a member of the firm since 1867.

Since the financial panic of 1907, the volume of business handled by the Works had been exceedingly fluctuating; and when the European war broke out in August, 1914, the Baldwin Plants were operating at only about one-third of their full capacity. The significance of the conflict was at once perceived by the officials of The Baldwin Locomotive Works, and the manufacturing facilities of the Company were promptly placed at the disposal of the Allied Governments.

The pressing needs for ordnance, ammunition and other supplies by France and Great Britain, were such that all efforts in these early days of the war were directed towards the development of armament and munitions. In Russia, however, greater distances and a desperate shortage of motive power and equipment necessitated the purchase of locomotives. Mr. S. M. Vauclain, then Vice-President of The Baldwin Locomotive Works, visited Russia in the fall of 1914 and also early in 1915, and was instrumental in securing a large part of this business. The first order thus obtained called for thirty Mallet locomotives of the 0-6-6-0 type, for the Vologda-Archangel Railway. These

MALLET ARTICULATED LOCOMOTIVE
For the Vologda-Archangel Railway, Russia

locomotives were of three feet, six inches gauge, and they were successfully and rapidly completed and shipped. One of them is illustrated on page 115. This order was followed by others, placed later by the Russian Government, and covering large

DECAPOD TYPE LOCOMOTIVE
For the Russian Government

numbers of heavy Decapod locomotives of five feet gauge, gasoline locomotives of seventy-five centimetres (2′ 5½″) gauge, gasoline trucks and gasoline tractors. The locomotives are illustrated on this page. One hundred of the Decapod locomotives, which could not be delivered in Russia because of the Bolshevik revolution, were subsequently purchased by the United States Government and so modified that they could be used temporarily on the railroads of the United States.

The gasoline locomotives were intended for trench service, a class of work for which they are well fitted, since as they emit no smoke they are comparatively inconspicuous.

GASOLINE LOCOMOTIVE
For the Russian Government

The French Government, late in the summer of 1914, sent a mission to the United States to make certain purchases. Early in November, 1914, the mission received cable instructions from France to purchase twenty tank locomotives of a gauge of sixty centimetres (1' 11⅞"), which were to be built to American designs and shipped as promptly as possible. The Baldwin Locomotive Works took this order on November 3rd, and the twenty locomotives, boxed and ready for shipment overseas, left the Works on November 21st. This was the beginning of a series of orders from the French Government which included both steam and gasoline locomotives totalling over one thousand in number. Among these were two-hundred and eighty locomotives of the Pechot type, designed for service on the narrow (sixty centimetres) gauge lines in the advanced areas. These locomotives were built throughout to the metric system of measurement, in accordance with designs furnished by the French Government. They are carried on two steam driven trucks or bogies, thus providing unusual flexibility and excellent tracking and riding qualities. The boiler has two fireboxes, placed in the middle between the bogies; and there is a separate boiler barrel, smokebox and stack at each end of the locomotive. The total weight in working order, with water-tanks and coal-boxes filled, is twenty-eight thousand one-hundred pounds. These locomotives were built during the years 1915 and 1916. The accompanying illustration represents the design.

The locomotives built for the British Government, for service similar to that performed by the Pechot locomotives, were of the

PECHOT TYPE LOCOMOTIVE
For the French Government

ten-wheeled (4-6-0) type with side tanks. A total of four-hundred and ninety-five of these were built during the latter part of 1916 and the Spring of 1917. The design generally followed American practice, as shown in the accompanying illustration; and the locomotives weighed, in working order, thirty-two thousand five hundred pounds each.

The British Government also received four hundred and sixty-five standard gauge locomotives of various types. Conspicuous among these were one hundred and fifty locomotives of the Consolidation (2-8-0) type, which were built in 1917. These locomotives had cylinders twenty-one inches in diameter by

TEN-WHEELED LOCOMOTIVE
For the British Government

twenty-eight inches stroke, and the weight in working order was one hundred and sixty-two thousand five hundred pounds.

The remainder of the standard gauge locomotives built for the British Government were of the 0-4-0, 0-6-0, 2-6-2 and 4-6-0 types. The last named had separate tenders, while the others were tank engines.

In addition to the locomotives built for strictly military purposes, large orders for Mikado (2-8-2) type freight locomotives were also received, during the war period, from two prominent French railways—the Paris, Lyons and Mediterranean, and the Nord. These locomotives were built throughout to the metric system, in accordance with specifications furnished by the purchasing companies. They use superheated steam and are of the balanced compound type, with inside high-pressure cylinders driving the second pair of coupled wheels and outside low-pressure cylinders driving the third pair. The total weight of one of these locomotives, exclusive of tender, is two hundred and two thousand pounds, of which the driving-wheels carry one hundred and forty-nine thousand four hundred pounds.

The construction of all of these locomotives for military service abroad, together with those ordered by domestic railways, soon placed the Works on a full capacity basis. Moreover, during this period orders were received from the British and French Governments for the machining of a large number of shells, varying in calibre from four and seven-tenths inches to twelve inches. These shells were manufactured in such of the locomotive shops as were available for the purpose, and also in new shops, specially built and equipped for this kind of work. The principal additions made to the Philadelphia plant were a four-story extension of the truck shop, measuring ninety by ninety-seven feet, and an eight-story building of re-enforced concrete, measuring ninety-eight feet six inches, by three hundred and ninety-six feet. A group of large shops one story in height, was also built at the Eddystone plant and utilized for the completion of the shell order from the French Government.

With the entrance of the United States into the war, in April, 1917, all industries manufacturing war supplies of any kind received a great stimulus. The presence of the American Army in France required the immediate construction of a great amount of motive power and rolling stock; and to meet the demand for locomotives, The Baldwin Locomotive Works were entrusted with what were probably the largest and most urgent orders ever placed in the history of locomotive building. The first of these orders was placed on July 17, 1917, and called for one hundred and fifty locomotives of the Consolidation (2-8-0) type. These locomotives, in general design, were similar to the Consolidation engines built for the British Government, the principal difference being that they were equipped with superheaters, whereas the British locomotives used saturated steam. The first of the locomotives for the United States Government was completed on August 10th, less than a month after the receipt of the order, and the last of the one hundred and fifty, on October 1st. These "Pershing Engines," as they became known, were subsequently

CONSOLIDATION TYPE LOCOMOTIVE
For the United States Government.   The first "Pershing Locomotive" built

ordered in large numbers; and when hostilities closed they were being shipped from the Works at the rate of three hundred per month.

Additional erecting capacity was required in order to handle all this work, and a second erecting shop, generally similar to that constructed in 1912, was built at Eddystone during the winter of 1917-1918.

Through the initiative of Mr. S. M. Felton, Director of Military Railways, and his mechanical aide, Colonel Milliken, an interesting method was developed of shipping the Pershing locomotives to France, erected complete with the exception of the headlight, smokestack and cab.   The locomotives and tenders were placed in the holds of the vessels on their own wheels, and after unloading them at St. Nazaire, France, comparatively little work was required before they were ready for service.   Much time and trouble were saved in this way.

In addition to the Pershing locomotives, narrow gauge steam locomotives of the 2-6-2 type, and gasoline locomotives of the

GASOLINE LOCOMOTIVE
For the United States Government

five, seven and one-half and twenty-five ton sizes, were also built for the United States Government. One of the gasoline locomotives, weighing seven and one-half tons, is illustrated on page 120.

On September 6, 1917, Mr. S. M. Vauclain was appointed Senior Vice-President of The Baldwin Locomotive Works, Mr. Grafton Greenough Vice-President in Charge of Sales, and Mr. John P. Sykes Vice-President in Charge of Manufacture.

Mr. Vauclain, as has been mentioned in these pages, had been connected with the Works since 1883. The great increase in the size and capacity of the plant which occurred during his term of service was due, to a large extent, to his untiring energy and to his exceptional ability as an organizer and executive. He also took an active interest in the development of the locomotive, and became recognized the world over as a locomotive expert and designer. It is safe to say that the production record made by the Works during the period of the war would not have been attained had it not been for his courage, energy and ability.

Mr. Greenough entered the service of the Company on December 28, 1885, as an employee of the Engineering Department. In August, 1899, he was transferred to the Operating Department in the capacity of Assistant Superintendent. At the time of the Louisiana Purchase Exposition in 1904 he was placed in charge of the St. Louis Office, later assuming charge of the sales organization in Philadelphia as General Sales Manager.

Mr. Sykes was apprenticed to The Baldwin Locomotive Works, entering service in 1879. He served in the capacities of Contractor, Assistant Foreman and General Foreman until 1905 when he was appointed Superintendent of the (then new) Eddystone Shops. In 1907 he left the parent company to become General Superintendent of the Standard Steel Works Company at Burnham, Pa., later returning to The Baldwin Locomotive Works as Assistant General Superintendent. In July, 1911, he was appointed General Superintendent, which position he held until his selection as Vice-President in Charge of Manufacture.

One of the most notable achievements of The Baldwin Locomotive Works during the war, was the building of a group of railway gun mounts for the United States Navy. These mounts carried fourteen-inch naval guns, which were available for shore service; and the original idea was to use them against a number of long-range German guns which were mounted near Ostend and firing into Dunkirk. The designs for the mounts were prepared at the Naval Gun Factory, Washington, under the direction of Captain A. L. Willard, Superintendent; Commander Harvey Delano, U. S. N., and George A. Chadwick, Chief Draftsman. When the designs were submitted to the bidders on January 25, 1918, Mr. S. M. Vauclain, who was then Chairman of the Munitions Committee of the War Industries Board, agreed that The Baldwin Locomotive Works would build the mounts, with the assistance of the American Bridge Company, in from one hundred to one hundred and twenty days. Five mounts were thereupon ordered; the first one, scheduled for delivery on May 15, 1918, was completed on April 25, while the last, which was scheduled for June 15, was completed May 25. Considering the fact that the design was new throughout, that there was a shortage of labor, and that many serious obstacles had to be overcome, this was an exceptionally creditable piece of work.

FOURTEEN-INCH RAILWAY GUN MOUNT

Each of these mounts is carried on twenty-four wheels, grouped in four trucks of six wheels each. The maximum firing elevation of the guns is forty-three degrees; but when firing at angles of fifteen degrees and upward, a structural steel foundation, surrounding a pit, is necessary, for the purpose of absorbing a portion of the shock and providing room for the recoil of the gun. These foundations were also supplied by The Baldwin Locomotive Works.

By the time the mounts were completed, conditions in Europe had changed to such an extent that it was impossible to send them to the Belgian Coast as first intended; hence they were shipped to the West Front, and were in service several weeks prior to the signing of the armistice. In all, the five batteries were fired seven hundred and eighty-two times on twenty-five different days, at ranges which averaged from thirty thousand to forty thousand yards; and while it was not possible, in the majority of cases, to make observations, it is known that severe damage was done.

These first five mounts were followed by six others, of similar construction; and after the signing of the armistice, the Works completed two additional mounts of an improved type, so designed that the gun can be fired at all angles without transferring the weight to a separate foundation. The new mounts were given thorough tests and proved highly satisfactory.

The Works also built thirty-eight caterpillar mounts, designed to carry seven-inch rifles. These were also constructed for the Navy, having been designed at the Naval Gun Factory. This type of mount has broad caterpillar treads, and can be run over rough roads and soft soil. In the field, these mounts are hauled about by tractors of one hundred and twenty horsepower.

In addition to building complete mounts, The Baldwin Locomotive Works constructed several styles of railway trucks for gun and howitzer mounts. At the time hostilities closed, preparations were being made for the manufacture, on a large scale, of heavy tanks equipped with Liberty motors. These were intended to destroy the wire defenses and machine gun nests put up by the Germans in their retreat. After the signing of the armistice, however, the order for these tanks was cancelled.

The war activities of The Baldwin Locomotive Works also included the construction of two large plants on their property at Eddystone for the manufacture of rifles and ammunition, and accomplishments in this connection constitute a series of achievements worthy of record.

On April 30, 1915, the British Government placed a contract

with the Remington Arms Company of Delaware for one million five hundred thousand rifles to be manufactured in one of the plants mentioned above, under the general direction of Mr. S. M. Vauclain. The work of constructing, equipping and organizing this enormous plant was fully accomplished, and production established by December 31, 1915, continuing until the close of 1918.

Mr. Charles H. Schlacks was engaged as General Manager on May 1, 1915, and to him great credit is due for the completion of the organization and the remarkable manufacturing results obtained.

The main building of the Rifle Plant covered fourteen acres of ground, and had a length of ten hundred and forty feet and a maximum width of eight hundred and sixteen feet. Great difficulty was experienced in obtaining delivery of equipment and machinery in time to meet the terms of the British contract, and some idea of the extent of the installation may be had from the fact that ten thousand machines, forty thousand two hundred feet of shafting, and four hundred and twenty-four thousand feet of belting were required.

The first British contract, mentioned above, was followed by another, signed August 2, 1915, and calling for five hundred thousand rifles, necessitated additional equipment. Because of the complexity of rifle manufacture, it was impossible to obtain experienced workmen; hence it was some time after the completion of the Plant before it could be operated at capacity. In consequence, an extension of time was granted for the completion of these contracts.

Soon after the United States entered the war, April 6, 1917, and in view of its prospective rifle requirements, cancellation of the British contracts, after the completion of six hundred thousand rifles, was arranged. Later, the British owned machinery and equipment passed by agreement to the United States Government who continued the British arrangement with the Remington Arms Company for its operation in the manufacture of rifles for the United States Army.

The first contract for rifles for the United States Government was signed on July 12, 1917; and during the twelve months

Eddystone Rifle Plant, Midvale Steel and Ordnance Co.

Plant of Eddystone Munitions Co.

beginning September, 1917, one million rifles were completed, the greatest known achievement in rifle production. These rifles differed slightly from those manufactured for the British Government, in that they fired a .300 calibre rimless cartridge; whereas the British rifle, which was an Enfield (model of 1914) fired a .303 calibre rim cartridge.

On January 2, 1918, the Remington Arms Company of Delaware was absorbed by the Midvale Steel and Ordnance Company (Eddystone Rifle Plant). The latter company operated the plant until after the close of the war.

The completion of rifle number one million for the United States Government was celebrated by a mass meeting held on September 23, 1918. The meeting was attended by a number of notable army, navy and industrial officials, and by more than fourteen thousand employees of the plant.

Operations at the plant ceased on January 11, 1919, at which time nearly three hundred thousand rifles were in process of manufacture. The Government then leased the premises for a storage plant.

The total number of rifles manufactured in this plant was one million nine hundred and fifty-nine thousand nine hundred and fifty-four, in addition to spare parts equivalent to two hundred thousand rifles. The greatest production exceeded six thousand rifles per day, and the maximum number of employees was fifteen thousand two hundred and ninety-four. When it is remembered that nearly two-thirds of all the rifles used in combat by the American Army in France were manufactured at Eddystone, the value of the work done can, to some extent, be appreciated; and the achievement was the more remarkable in view of the exceptional difficulties encountered in equipping the plant and securing labor and material.

The second plant referred to was built primarily for the production of Russian ammunition ordered by the British Government. Early in 1915, Messrs. J. P. Morgan and Company, representing His Britannic Majesty's Government, were requested to negotiate with American manufacturers for the production of three-inch Russian shrapnel, and Mr. S. M. Vauclain made a tentative agreement for the manufacture of two million five hundred thousand of such shells. As the Charter of The Baldwin Locomotive Works did not permit it to handle explosives, the Eddystone Ammunition Corporation was formed on June 10, 1915, for the purpose of carrying out the contract.

The new Company was organized with S. M. Vauclain as Managing Director, Andrew Fletcher as President, Captain Walter M. Wilhelm as Vice-President and General Manager, and John P. Sykes as Consulting Manager. The stock of the Company was held and owned outside of The Baldwin Locomotive Works because of provisions in the Charter to which previous reference has been made.

A contract, calling for two million five hundred thousand rounds of three-inch Russian artillery ammunition with shrapnel shells, was executed on July 23, 1915, for completion by December 31, 1916. Work was immediately started on the construction of the plant, which was located along the river front on what was originally swamp lands. The main buildings consisted of two shops each four hundred and fifty by seven hundred and fifty feet, connected to an office building fifty by four hundred and fifty feet, which was placed between them. These buildings were of steel and tile construction, two stories high; the upper floors of the shop buildings being removable, so that cranes could be subsequently installed for after-war production. A large number of smaller structures, which were used for powder loading buildings, storehouses, magazines, etc., were also erected. The office building was completed and occupied November first.

In connection with this plant, a modern wharf was built along the Delaware River front. This wharf was equipped with a fifty-ton gantry crane, and had a minimum depth of thirty feet of water alongside, so that large cargo steamers could dock and load.

Some difficulty was experienced in equipping the plant, and much of the heavy machinery was manufactured by The Baldwin Locomotive Works since it could not be obtained elsewhere. In addition to this, The Baldwin Locomotive Works installed the heat-treating plant and supervised its operation.

Additional time was allowed on the contracts, and the order was finally completed on August 10, 1917.

In connection with this work the Eddystone Ammunition Corporation secured the contract for proving Russian ammunition of their own and other makes, and a proving ground for this purpose was established at Lakehurst, New Jersey, with Captain C. K. Rockwell in charge, who distinguished himself in overcoming what appeared to be insurmountable difficulties in record time.

By this arrangement the Eddystone Ammunition Corporation were required to test ammunition for other manufacturers, and lots representing some seven million six hundred thousand of three-inch Russian shrapnel and high explosive shells with their component parts were tested.

The work done at the proving ground was of the greatest value, and was an unqualified success. The last shot was fired December 24, 1917.

The work done in the plant of the Eddystone Ammunition Corporation was necessarily of a dangerous character, and while every precaution was taken to safe-guard the workers, there was one serious disaster. On April 10, 1917, four days after the United States declared war on Germany, an explosion occurred in "F" building, a loading shop isolated from the main building on account of the large amount of powder used. The building was completely demolished, and one hundred and twenty-eight people were killed, while a large number of others were injured. Heroic work was done at the rescue, both by employees and also by outsiders who happened to be in the vicinity and who could reach the spot. The cause of the explosion has never been determined.

In May, 1917, the United States Government requested the Eddystone Ammunition Corporation to submit a proposition covering the manufacture of a large amount of three-inch shrapnel. Because of British and Russian interests represented, however, the proposed program could not be accepted by the Directors of the Corporation. After some negotiation, the United States Government agreed to purchase the machinery and equipment of the Eddystone Ammunition Corporation; and The Baldwin Locomotive Works, the owners of the buildings, organized a subsidiary company to manufacture the shrapnel. This subsidiary was organized on September 27, 1917, as the Eddystone Munitions Company.

The officers of the Company were as follows:—

Charles H. Schlacks, Chairman of the Board.

James McNaughton, President.

Captain Walter M. Wilhelm, Vice-President.

J. L. Tate, Secretary and Treasurer.

W. C. Stagg, Assistant Secretary and Treasurer.

For nearly a year previous to the organization of the Eddystone Munitions Company, Mr. McNaughton had been directing the affairs of the Eddystone Ammunition Corporation as personal representative of Mr. Vauclain. He was thus peculiarly well qualified to assume the presidency of the new Company. On October 1, 1917, he was also appointed Consulting Vice-President of The Baldwin Locomotive Works.

The original order, placed by the United States Government, called for seven hundred and fifty thousand complete rounds of three-inch shrapnel. After the work had been started, the size of the shells was changed to seventy-five millimetres, which materially retarded delivery. Difficulty was experienced in maintaining the output of these shells, on account of failure to receive the component parts promptly.

On April 1, 1918, a contract was signed for one million seventy-five millimetre high explosive shells. The cartridge case shop, in the meantime, was manufacturing cartridge cases of high quality at the rate of sixty thousand per week. In addition there were loaded, assembled and packed over one million six hundred thousand rounds of seventy-five millimetre shrapnel, the component parts of which were furnished by the Government.

During the early months of 1918 the Government also ordered large quantities of various kinds of fuses, boosters and adapters, necessitating a number of changes in the shop lay-out and the installation of new machinery. This was accomplished, however, in an incredibly short space of time.

In addition to the work for the United States Government, a contract was made with the British Government for five hundred thousand six-inch high explosive shells. The armistice was signed before this contract was finished, but four hundred and seventy-five thousand of the shells were actually completed, the maximum production reaching four thousand two hundred per day.

The epidemic of influenza, which swept the country early in the fall of 1918, seriously affected the work of the Company on account of the great amount of illness among the employees. Among the first to succumb was Captain Walter M. Wilhelm, Vice-President, who died on October third. This was a severe loss, as owing to his wide experience in the manufacture of .munitions, his services were of exceptional value.

The maximum number of employees of the Eddystone Munitions Company was six thousand five hundred and eighty-three, and the average number four thousand two hundred and thirteen. The labor situation presented many problems, due to the heavy labor turn-over and the difficulty of securing skilled workers. Excellent wages, backed by a bonus system and considerate, tactful management, did much to hold employees who would otherwise have sought employment elsewhere.

After the signing of the armistice, on November 11, 1918, production rapidly slackened, and on December 31st of that year manufacturing ceased. The machinery and equipment were sold, and the buildings turned over to The Baldwin Locomotive Works, to be subsequently re-equipped as locomotive shops.

An idea of the extent of the war activities of The Baldwin Locomotive Works and its associated companies, may be obtained from the following summary of material supplied to the Allied Nations and the United States:

Locomotives built..........................5551
Gun Mounts (seven and fourteen-inch)......51
Foundations for fourteen-inch mounts.......20
Trucks for gun and howitzer mounts........5 sets
Total number of shells (including those manu-
    factured by Eddystone Ammunition Cor-
    poration and Eddystone Munitions Com-
    pany)..............................6,565,355
Cartridge cases................................1,863,900
Miscellaneous ammunition items...............1,905,213

The aggregate value of the war contracts executed and

delivered by The Baldwin Locomotive Works, the Standard Steel Works Company, the Eddystone Ammunition Corporation, and the Eddystone Munitions Company, was approximately $250,000,000.

In connection with the war activities of The Baldwin Locomotive Works, it should be recorded, as a matter of historical interest, that among those lost on board the Cunard steamer "Lusitania," when that vessel was torpedoed by a German submarine on May 7, 1915, were W. Sterling Hodges and his family. Mr. Hodges, at the time, was en route for Paris, where he was to act as one of the representatives of The Baldwin Locomotive Works.

While the greater part of the product of the Works, during the war, was for military purposes, a record should also be made of a number of interesting locomotives for railway service. At the Panama-Pacific International Exposition, held in San Francisco during 1915, an exhibit of five steam locomotives was presented as follows:

A Mikado type locomotive for the Southern Pacific Co.;

A locomotive of similar construction for the San Pedro, Los Angeles and Salt Lake R. R.;

A Pacific type locomotive for the Atchison, Topeka & Santa Fe Ry.;

A Santa Fe type locomotive for the Chicago, Burlington & Quincy R. R., and a stock locomotive of the Mikado type designed for logging service. Two electric trucks were also exhibited; and an exhibit, made by the McCloud River R. R., included a Baldwin locomotive built for that line. The Works received the Grand Prize for locomotives and electric trucks.

MOUNTAIN TYPE LOCOMOTIVE
For the Jamaica Government Railways

In July, 1916, the first locomotives of the Mountain (4-8-2) type to be built by The Baldwin Locomotive Works, were completed. They were of standard gauge, for the Jamaica Government Rys. The illustration on page 131 shows the general design. This type of locomotive was subsequently built in considerable numbers, for heavy passenger service in the United States.

The Government assumed control of all the trunk line railways of the United States, December 28, 1917, at a time when the various lines were taxed to their capacity. The operation of the railways was intrusted to the United States Railroad Administration, which body immediately assumed the right to centralize the purchases of all railroad equipment, including locomotives. The Director General of the Railroad Administration immediately appointed a committee to standardize the specifications for locomotives and in accordance with his ruling, that committee and a committee of railway officials collaborated with the representatives of the locomotive builders in preparing twelve specifications and designs of locomotives comprising twelve sizes of engines divided among eight types. The locomotive builders sharing in this work were The Baldwin Locomotive Works, the American Locomotive Company and the Lima Locomotive Works, Incorporated. The first conference was held at the office of The Baldwin Locomotive Works, March 13, 14 and 15, 1918, and subsequent meetings were held in the Interstate Commerce Building, Washington, with the result that an order for standard locomotives was placed and divided among the three builders April 30, 1918, and subsequent orders were placed with the last two companies named. Some locomotives of each of the twelve standard specifications were built by both The Baldwin Locomotive Works and the American Locomotive Company, whereas the activities of the Lima Locomotive Works were confined to two types of engines.

The standard locomotives were distributed to the various railroads of the country as directed by the Railroad Administration, and it will be interesting to note if the lower costs of locomotives made possible through standardization can overcome, in the mind of the railroad world, the advantages which may be obtained through the use of locomotives particularly designed and adapted to the individual service of the railroads on which they operate.

ONE OF THE UNITED STATES GOVERNMENT STANDARD LOCOMOTIVES
Heavy Mikado Type

Only one order for standard locomotives was placed with these Works, because the capacity of the plant was practically absorbed by the Government's demand for Military Railway locomotives and for military and naval equipment.

Locomotive Number 50,000 was completed in September, 1918. This engine is of the Mallet type, with 2-8-8-2 wheel arrangement, and is one of a group of twelve, specially designed for service on the Appalachia Division of the Southern Ry. System. These locomotives had been ordered before the standardization program was decided upon. Locomotive number 50,000

MALLET ARTICULATED LOCOMOTIVE
For the Southern Railway.   Baldwin Locomotive No. 50,000

is equipped with a superheater and mechanical stoker, and weighs, in working order, four hundred and twenty-seven thousand pounds, exclusive of tender. The accompanying illustration represents the design.

When the armistice was signed and it became necessary to turn attention to the problems of peace, it was found that the removal of war business, however gradually accomplished, would reveal a lack of balance in the general organization of the Works.

As a consequence of this business being obtained direct from the United States and Allied Governments, the Commercial and Financial Departments remained undeveloped, while the Industrial Department had been enormously increased to take care of the emergencies of war. This lack of balance was particularly noticeable in the Sales Department, as war work had been obtained with practically no solicitation.

In adjusting to meet the new conditions, it was obviously necessary to expand the Commercial Organization so as to be able to obtain the business necessary for greatly enlarged shops and manufacturing facilities. The opportunity for sales was especially attractive in foreign countries where Germany, formerly the most active competitor, had lost ground.

In order to inaugurate a more vigorous selling campaign, the Sales Department, in March, 1919, was reorganized, and two distinct departments were created—a Domestic Sales Department and a Foreign Sales Department. The long established Extra Work Department, with its record of past successes, was abolished; and the work formerly committed to its care was divided between the two Sales Departments. Mr. Grafton Greenough, formerly Vice-President in Charge of Sales, was made Vice-President in Charge of Domestic Sales. Mr. Francois de St. Phalle, who had been connected with the Works since 1903, and who during the war had acted as Manager of Munitions, was appointed Vice-President in Charge of Foreign Sales. Both departments were organized on the basis of zone management, with sections especially devoted to sales in certain determined districts and countries. Twelve direct Baldwin offices were opened in foreign countries, and men of the highest capacity selected and equipped to act as Baldwin Managers in those countries.

On May 19, 1919, Mr. Alba B. Johnson resigned from the presidency. Mr. Johnson first entered the service of the Works as junior clerk on May 14, 1877. He left the following year to enter the employment of the Edge Moor Iron Works of Wilmington, Delaware, returning to The Baldwin Locomotive Works on September 1, 1879. From that time until his resignation, he served the Works continuously; first as assistant to Mr. John H.

Converse, as a member of the firm of Burnham, Williams and Company from January 1, 1896; as Vice-President and Treasurer from July 1, 1909, and finally as President from July 1, 1911. Mr. Johnson's contribution to the success of The Baldwin Locomotive Works was steady and important throughout these many years. His efforts to develop the foreign business of the Company were untiring, and his abilities in the executive capacities in which he was engaged were strengthened by an exceptional memory for the facts of important transactions throughout the period of his long service.

Mr. Johnson was succeeded as President by Mr. S. M. Vauclain. He continued to serve, however, as a member of the Board of Directors.

On May 19, 1919, Mr. William de Krafft was appointed Vice-President in Charge of Finance, and Treasurer. Mr. de Krafft had been connected with the Works since March 29, 1895. After serving in a number of the shop offices, he was transferred to the Purchasing Department, and subsequently to the Financial Department in the Main office. When the Company was first incorporated, on July 1, 1909, Mr. de Krafft was appointed Secretary and Assistant Treasurer. At the time of the second incorporation, July 1, 1911, he was appointed Secretary and Treasurer, which position he held until his appointment as Vice-President.

Two orders of special interest, which were filled for export during the winter of 1919-1920, called respectively for one hundred and fifty locomotives for the Polish Government and thirty for the South African Railways. The Polish locomotives are of standard gauge, and are practically duplicates of the "Pershing" Consolidation engines previously described. The South African locomotives are of three feet six inches gauge, and are of the Mountain (4-8-2) type. They have a total weight, exclusive of tender, of two hundred and five thousand pounds, and are of exceptional capacity in view of the narrow gauge and the restricted clearance limits imposed. They were built in accordance with drawings and specifications furnished by the railway, and the design incorporates plate frames and various other special features. One of these locomotives is illustrated herewith.

MOUNTAIN TYPE LOCOMOTIVE, SOUTH AFRICAN RAILWAYS

In this connection, special reference should be made to the shipping and receiving facilities, both domestic and foreign, which have been developed by The Baldwin Locomotive Works. The Eddystone Plant, where locomotives are erected and prepared for shipment, has track connection with three important railways. The Washington main line and a branch of the Pennsylvania Railroad system, the main line of the Baltimore & Ohio Railroad, and the Philadelphia & Reading Railway all run directly to the plant, and connect with a system of industrial railways covering all material yards, shops and docks. The Baldwin Locomotive Works is thus not only fitted with full facilities for railway and deep water shipping, but also for the receiving of materials direct from all parts of the country or from foreign ports.

The Eddystone Plant is located on the west bank of the Delaware River about fourteen miles below the City of Philadelphia, which stands second to New York only among the ports of the United States, the total movement of freight through the port in 1919 amounting to 9,314,755 tons. To accommodate this traffic the Delaware has been dredged to provide a ship channel eight hundred feet in width and thirty-five feet in depth at low water. At Eddystone the channel lies about two thousand feet off shore. In 1915, when the port facilities at Eddystone were planned, Crum Creek, about one hundred and fifty feet wide and from two to six feet deep, flowed through the land selected as the development site, which was low and marshy, being under water at high tide. In general terms the project contemplated the diversion of Crum Creek to a new channel farther to the northward, the reclamation of the marshy area through which it formerly flowed, the construction upon the reclaimed land of a system of wharves with suitable storage yards and railroad

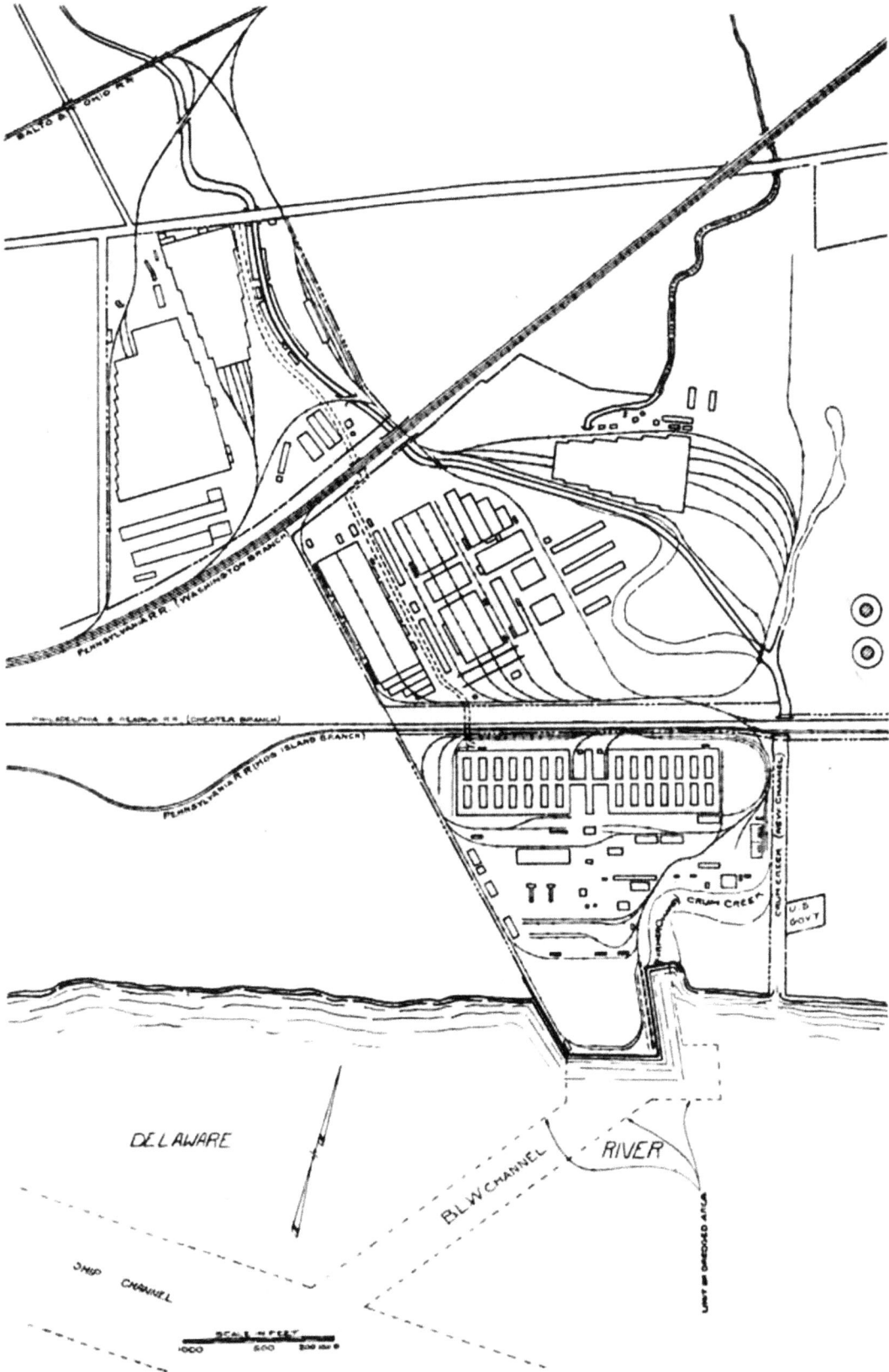

PLAN VIEW OF EDDYSTONE PLANT, 1920, SHOWING RAILROAD CONNECTIONS AND
DOCKING FACILITIES

connections, and the provision of a turning basin and a dredged channel affording access from the wharves to the ship channel as well as ample space for maneuvering vessels at the docks.

Reference to the plan of the Eddystone Works as thus far developed, which appears on page 137, will serve to fix in mind the features of this installation as well as the general layout of the plant and its location with reference to the railroads running through or adjacent to it.

Mention has been made of the wharf built during the War, adjoining the plant which was leased to the Eddystone Ammunition Corporation. The north-east front of this wharf is five hundred and sixty feet long, and is served by a gantry portal crane of fifty tons capacity. The south-east front, six hundred and forty feet in length, is used for package freight which can be loaded by ship's tackle. Both fronts are served by adequate trackage. A turning basin eleven hundred feet in diameter, and having a minimum depth of thirty feet of water, is located alongside the wharf. This basin communicates with the main ship channel by a connecting channel three hundred feet wide, having a minimum depth of twenty-two feet at low tide, and a maximum depth of twenty-eight at high tide. Sea-going steamers can thus be loaded at the plant, for direct shipment to any foreign port.

These docking facilities, which will be increased as occasion requires, constitute the nucleus of a modern loading port at Eddystone. They have been provided in accordance with the policy of the Works to offer the most improved and complete service possible. The Branch Offices and Agencies of the Company, listed on page 144, are so located as to cover the world's territory to the best possible advantage, and are prepared to render the most prompt and efficient service. This service includes the superintendence of shipment under the expert and individual attention of a specially organized shipping department and the erection and trial of locomotives on arrival at their destination.

The illustration on page 139, shows the loading of locomotives on the steamship "Kosciuszko," and is interesting for the reason that this vessel flies the flag of the recently formed Polish Republic, and was the first steamer of Polish registry to clear

Loading the Steamer "Kosciusko"—The First Steamer Flying the Flag of the Republic of Poland to Visit Any American Port

from any American port. She docked at Eddystone, December 1, 1919, and departed December 11, having loaded twelve locomotives for the Polish Government. Shortly thereafter she sailed direct for Danzig, the newly acquired Polish port. The engraving below shows a small part of the river frontage, with two steamers docked for loading. On page 141, is shown a portion of the wharf served by the gantry crane and piled high with packing cases ready for shipment.

STEAMERS MOORED AT THE EDDYSTONE WHARVES

Philadelphia's location is peculiarly favorable, in that it is in proximity to the principal coal mining and steel manufacturing sections of the country. The city, moreover, has a large permanent population of skilled mechanics, engaged in machine and engine building, thus giving an abundant force of expert workmen from which to draw when necessary.

The Works are fully equipped to build all types of locomotives and to supply locomotive duplicate and repair parts of every description. With the exception of the boiler and tank plates,

ON THE WHARF AT EDDYSTONE, SHOWING PACKING CASES READY FOR SHIPMENT

chilled wheels, boiler tubes and special patented appliances, all parts of locomotives and tenders are made in the main or adjunct plants from the raw materials. The Works are also prepared to furnish such general engineering supplies and equipment as can be manufactured in a large locomotive building plant.

Beginning with "Old Ironsides," built in 1831-32, consecutive construction numbers have been applied to the locomotives built at these Works. The growth of the business is indicated by the following statement, giving the years for the completion of locomotives numbered in even thousands:

No. 1,000, 1861	No. 13,000, 1892	No. 25,000, 1905
" 2,000, 1869	" 14,000, 1894	" 26,000, 1905
" 3,000, 1872	" 15,000, 1896	" 27,000, 1905
" 4,000, 1876	" 16,000, 1898	" 28,000, 1906
" 5,000, 1880	" 17,000, 1899	" 29,000, 1906
" 6,000, 1882	" 18,000, 1900	" 30,000, 1907
" 7,000, 1883	" 19,000, 1901	" 31,000, 1907
" 8,000, 1886	" 20,000, 1902	" 32,000, 1907
" 9,000, 1888	" 21,000, 1902	" 33,000, 1908
" 10,000, 1889	" 22,000, 1903	" 34,000, 1909
" 11,000, 1890	" 23,000, 1903	" 35,000, 1910
" 12,000, 1891	" 24,000, 1904	" 36,000, 1911

No. 37,000, 1911   No. 43,000, 1916   No. 49,000, 1918
"   38,000, 1912   "   44,000, 1916   "   50,000, 1918
"   39,000, 1912   "   45,000, 1917   "   51,000, 1918
"   40,000, 1913   "   46,000, 1917   "   52,000, 1919
"   41,000, 1913   "   47,000, 1917   "   53,000, 1920
"   42,000, 1915   "   48,000, 1918

The production during the years 1866-1919 was as follows:

Year	Locomotives	Year	Locomotives	Year	Locomotives
1866	118	1884	429	1902	1533
1867	127	1885	242	1903	2022
1868	124	1886	550	1904	1485
1869	235	1887	653	1905	2250
1870	280	1888	737	1906	2666
1871	331	1889	827	1907	2655
1872	422	1890	946	1908	617
1873	437	1891	899	1909	1024
1874	205	1892	731	1910	1675
1875	130	1893	772	1911	1606
1876	232	1894	313	1912	1618
1877	185	1895	401	1913	2061
1878	292	1896	547	1914	804
1879	298	1897	501	1915	867
1880	517	1898	755	1916	1989
1881	554	1899	901	1917	2737
1882	563	1900	1217	1918	3580
1883	557	1901	1375	1919	1722

The present organization, based upon an annual capacity of three thousand five hundred locomotives, is as follows:

Number of men employed		21,500
Hours of labor, per man, per day		10
Principal departments run continuously, hours per day		23
Horse-power employed { Steam engines		16,700
{ Oil engines		3,400
Electric power purchased (horse-power)		8,500
Number of buildings comprised in the Works		137
Acreage comprised in the Works { Philadelphia		19.33
{ Eddystone		595.65
Acreage of floor space comprised in buildings		143

Horse-power of electric motors employed for power
    transmission, aggregate....................   57,400
Number of incandescent electric lamps in service..   14,000
Number of electric motors in service...........   3,450
Consumption of coal, in net tons, per week, about   4,200
     "   " fuel oil, in gallons, per week, about   175,000
     "   " iron and steel, in net tons, per
    week, about.............................   6,500
Consumption of other materials, in net tons, per
    week, about.............................   3,000

The future holds out many prospects of trade expansion, and The Baldwin Locomotive Works are fully prepared to meet any demands, either domestic or foreign, which may be made upon them.

The Baldwin Locomotive Works

General Offices of the Company

500 North Broad Street, Philadelphia

REPRESENTATIVES AND AGENTS

New York, N. Y.	RICHARD SANDERSON	120 Broadway
Chicago, Ill.	CHARLES RIDDELL	627 Railway Exchange
St. Louis, Mo.	A. S. GOBLE	1210 Boatmen's Bank Building
Richmond, Va.	G. F. JONES	407 Travelers Building
Pittsburgh, Pa.	E. CONVERSE PEIRCE	279 Union Arcade Building
Houston, Texas	PAUL G. CHEATHAM	401 Carter Building
St. Paul, Minn.	HENRY BLANCHARD	908 Merchants National Bank Building
Portland, Ore.	A. J. BEUTER	312 Northwestern Bank Building
San Francisco, Cal.	WILLIAMS, DIMOND & CO.	310 Sansome Street
Argentine Republic	WALLACE R. LEE	Buenos Aires, Paseo Colon 185
Balkan States	E. ST.J. GREBLE	Bucharest, Roumania
Brazil	C. H. CRAWFORD	Rio de Janeiro, Rua Alfandega, 5
Brazil	CORY BROS. & CO., LTD.	Bahia
Brazil	EDWARD C. HOLDEN	Para
Brazil	MONTEATH & CO.	Pernambuco
Chile	WESSEL, DUVAL & CO.	Valparaiso
China	ANDERSEN, MEYER & CO., LTD.	Shanghai
Dutch East Indies	J. O. FEENSTRA	Bandoeng, Java
France	H. A. F. CAMPBELL	Paris, 14 Rue Duphot
Great Britain	R. P. C. SANDERSON	London, 34 Victoria Street, S. W. 1
Hawaiian Islands	C. BREWER & CO., LTD.	Honolulu
Japan	SALE & FRAZAR, LTD.	Tokio
Mexico	CARL HOLT SMITH	Mexico City
New South Wales	R. TOWNS & CO.	Sydney
New Zealand	PHILIPS & PIKE	Wellington
Peru	C. R. CULLEN	Lima
Poland	FRANK W. MORSE	Warsaw, Krolewska, 1
Porto Rico and Santo Domingo	R. CARRION	San Juan, American Colonial Bank Building
Portugal	E. PINTO BASTO & CO., LTD.	Lisbon
Portuguese East Africa	MANN, GEORGE & CO., LTD.	Lourenco Marques, Delagoa Bay
Scandinavia	OLAV BELSHEIM	Christiania, Norway (Toldbogaden, 8)
Southern Africa	F. V. GREEN	Johannesburg
Spain	H. P. AUSTIN	Madrid, Apartado 473
Victoria	NEWELL & CO.	Melbourne
Western Australia	LESLIE & CO.	Perth
West Indies	G. R. PEREZ	Havana, 520 National Bank of Cuba Building

HISTORY

OF THE

Standard Steel Works Company

STANDARD STEEL WORKS CO.

OFFICES:
500 North Broad Street, Philadelphia, Pa.

WORKS: Burnham, Pa.

TRADE MARK

DIRECTORS

ALBA B. JOHNSON, Rosemont, Pa.

SAMUEL M. VAUCLAIN, Rosemont, Pa.

SYDNEY E. HUTCHINSON, Philadelphia, Pa.

SIDNEY F. TYLER, Philadelphia, Pa.

B. DAWSON COLEMAN, Lebanon, Pa.

ARTHUR W. SEWALL, Philadelphia, Pa.

ARTHUR E. NEWBOLD, Philadelphia, Pa.

OFFICERS

ARTHUR E. NEWBOLD	Chairman of the Board
SAMUEL M. VAUCLAIN	President
ROBERT RADFORD	Vice-President and Treasurer
A. A. STEVENSON	Vice-President and Engineer
WM. H. PUGH, JR.	Secretary
A. B. EHST	Comptroller

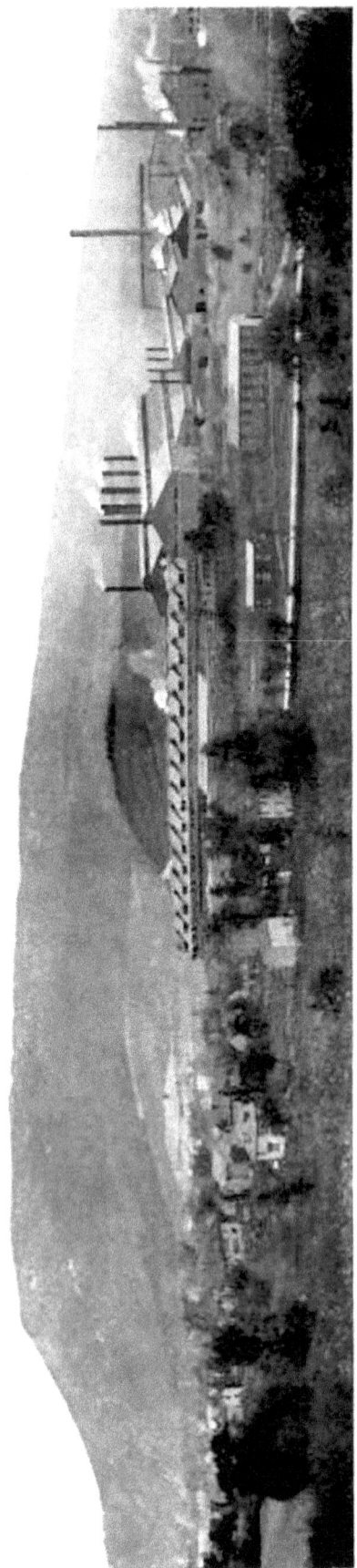

North End of Plant

South End of Plant

STANDARD STEEL WORKS, BURNHAM, PA.

HISTORY

OF THE

Standard Steel Works Company

The executive offices of the Standard Steel Works Company are located at 500 North Broad Street, Philadelphia, Pennsylvania. The Works are situated at Burnham, on the Kishacoquillas Creek, about three miles from Lewistown, Mifflin County, Pennsylvania; a locality long identified with the iron and steel industry.

The land on which the Works are built is part of a tract originally warranted by Everhart Martin on April 2, 1755. Two hundred and twenty-five acres of the original warrant were sold to George Hanawalt on July 4, 1795, for £1000. A forge was established in 1795 by William Brown and William Maclay, who petitioned the Court in August, 1795, for "a road from Freedom Forge by the nearest and best way to the River Juniata, near to or at McClelland's Landing." In 1811 Freedom Forge was acquired by Joseph Martin, Samuel Miller and John Brown, who operated under the name of Miller, Martin and Company. In 1827 John Norris purchased the interests of William Brown, but resold it in 1833 to William Brown, Jr. The Plant was used until 1834, when it was rebuilt with "one chafery and six refinery fires" having a capacity of "eight hundred tons of blooms per annum."

In 1847 the forge and furnace portion of the property was purchased by Archibald Wright, John Wright and John A. Wright, Philadelphia. In 1856 Messrs. Wright transferred the property to the "Freedom Iron Company" with Joseph Thomas as President. A tire mill with a capacity of two thousand tires a year was added. In 1865 the Company installed two five-ton Bessemer converters and rail mill, and built the Emma Furnace with the intention of using the "Stone Creek" ores to supply the Bessemer plant. The first heat was blown May 1, 1868. A tire mill and a double acting ten-ton steam hammer were imported from England. The use of the native ores proved unsuccessful, and in 1870 the Bessemer plant was sold, some of the machinery being removed to Joliet, Illinois, some to Johnstown, Pennsylvania, and the remainder becoming the property of the Logan Iron and Steel Company.

In 1870 William Butcher leased the tire mill and hammer and the building erected for the Bessemer plant, and began the manufacture of crucible steel tires. William Butcher took with him from Philadelphia forty men for tire rollers, hammermen and machinists. Some of these men who manufactured the first steel tires made in America are still (1920) in the employ of the Standard Steel Works.

The following year he failed, his creditors carrying on the business until 1875, when they organized The Standard Steel Works, which was incorporated in that year. The Standard Steel Works purchased the property in 1895. The manufacture of crucible steel tires was continued for some years. With the advent of acid open-hearth steel for tires an arrangement was made with the Otis Steel Company, then the leading manufacturer of steel, under which tires were produced from Otis steel ingots. This partnership continued until, realizing the necessity of producing their own steel, the Company established a complete melting plant, from which the first heat was poured March 19, 1895. This furnace, which had a capacity of fifteen tons, was the first rolling open-hearth furnace to be put

STEEL TIRED WHEEL WITH PLATE CENTER

into operation. It was served by an electric-driven charging machine, which was the first of its kind to be used, and is still in operation.

The manufacture of built-up steel tired wheels for engine trucks, coaches, tenders and industrial purposes was begun in 1892. The centers were made of wrought or cast iron, and later cast steel centers were added.

In 1895 the Company designed and introduced the bolted type of steel tired wheel, which has proved to be the best type for all purposes. It has been adopted by many railroads, to the extent that other types of tire fastening have become practically obsolete. The bolted type was adopted by the Master Car Builders' Association in June, 1912, as the standard M. C. B. type of tire fastening.

In 1911 the Company introduced the rolled steel center, placing five hundred such centers with bolted type tires in the Pullman service. Since then the majority of steel tired wheels have been fitted with rolled steel centers.

STEEL TIRED WHEEL WITH SPOKE CENTER

The demand for steel castings being in excess of the supply, a steel foundry was established in 1897 with two fifteen-ton open-hearth furnaces, which furnaces have since been rebuilt as stationary furnaces of twenty tons capacity. The demand for steel castings kept increasing, so that it was necessary in 1910 to erect No. 2 Steel Foundry, which doubled the capacity.

As the demand for locomotive forgings was in evidence the Company built a Forge Shop in 1898. It was necessary to enlarge in 1902; and in 1916, under the stress of war conditions, its capacity and scope were increased by the installation of seven steam hydraulic presses. At the present time (1920) the Company is equipped with a plant of the most modern type, and is able to produce locomotive and marine forgings, shafts, rolls, ordnance forgings and miscellaneous forgings of weights up to forty tons, which can be handled under presses or hammers.

During the year 1900 plans for the systematic enlargement of every department of the Standard Steel Works were instituted. The bed of the Kishacoquillas Creek was changed to allow uninterrupted space for additional buildings.

The advent of new and greater activities necessitated the installation of increased facilities for the greater production of steel. Consequently, in 1902 Open-Hearth Plant No. 2 was built with one fifty-ton open-hearth furnace. Another fifty-ton open-hearth furnace was added in 1905, a third in 1907, a fourth in 1910 and a fifth in 1916. Open-Hearth Plant No. 3 was built in 1917 with two seventy-five-ton open-hearth furnaces. The capacity at this time (1920) is approximately two hundred thousand tons annually.

SOLID FORGED AND ROLLED STEEL WHEEL

Previous to 1903 the Company operated a small iron foundry for the production of its own cast iron wheel centers and miscellaneous castings for its own work. In 1903 two large iron foundries were built for the manufacture of miscellaneous castings. Since then the Company has utilized the foundries for the production of their own centers, ingot moulds and other castings required for their own use, and malleable iron for the trade.

In 1903 a Spring Shop was built with machinery of the latest and most approved design, especially constructed to meet requirements of this particular class of manufacture. It has been kept modern with the most up-to-date machinery to supply the most exacting demands.

In 1904 the manufacture of the "Standard" solid forged and rolled steel wheels was begun. This was the introduction of this type of wheel into America, and it was at that time offered as a substitute for the cast iron chilled wheel which had become inadequate for modern service. The demand for rolled wheels to replace cast iron chilled wheels under the lightest as well as the heaviest equipment constantly increased, so that in 1910 a second plant was erected, doubling the capacity. In order to meet the increased demands in 1917, a third mill was erected. The preliminary forging operations for this mill are performed on two four-cylinder hydraulic presses of ten thousand tons capacity, especially designed for the work. The furnaces in this mill are heated by pulverized coal supplied from a central pulverizing station.

Realizing the necessity of improving the steel in every possible manner in order to meet the most exacting demands, the subject of heat treatment has been given careful consideration and extensive experiments have been carried on. In 1910 a large heating plant was built, with further extensive additions in 1911. In 1916 the plant was doubled in capacity and provided with vertical tanks that were required for annealing, quenching, and tempering of gun and howitzer forgings, which were supplied by the Company to the United States Government. The furnaces are equipped with accurate pyrometer control.

The weight of electric equipment and the severity of service were constantly increasing so that cast steel gears and pinions were neither rendering adequate service, nor could they meet the demands imposed upon them. In 1911, therefore, the Company began the manufacture of forged steel gears, which have met all expectations and proved very successful.

The production of the various products necessarily meant constant increase in machine shop capacity, so that now the main shop is one hundred and seventy-five feet wide by ten hundred and fifty feet long, containing horizontal boring mills for machining tires, wheels and driving-wheel centers, with additional equipment of lathes, planers and other tools for finishing heavy forgings; and equipped with specially designed lathes for hollow boring of driving-axles, wrist pins, etc.

Among the specialties produced by the Company, particular mention must be made of built-up crank axles for locomotives. This type of crank axle was originally designed to meet the requirements of the four-cylinder balanced compound locomotive.

Solid forged crank axles are in extensive use in Europe, but for lighter locomotives than are used in America. Even with the lighter locomotives, the solid cranks have not proved entirely satisfactory. In addition to the axle designed by the Company for use in the United States, the Company during the war designed and supplied a large number of crank axles built on the same general principle but of different pattern. The majority of these axles were built up of nine pieces, while others were made in five pieces, the crank-pins and central web being made from a single quenched and tempered forging.

The Standard Steel Works met the demands imposed upon it by the extraordinary conditions caused by the World War.

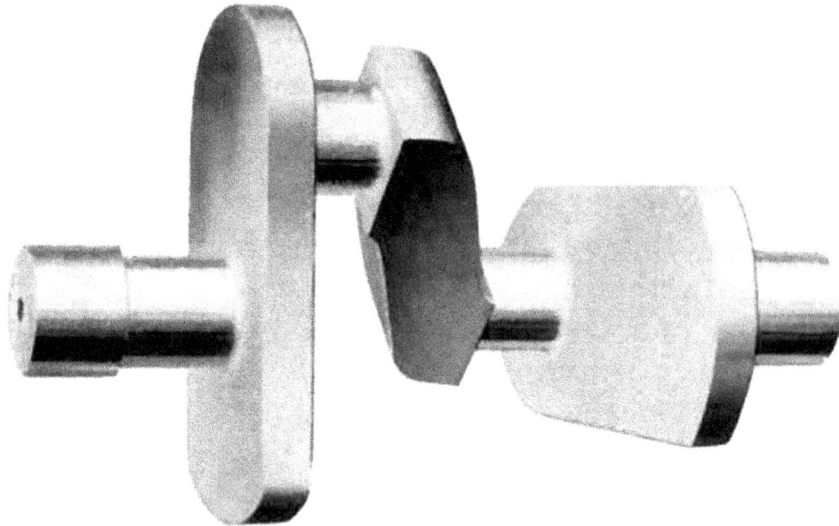

FIVE-PIECE LOCOMOTIVE CRANK AXLE

It was found necessary to maintain a full volume of output and at the same time to develop and manufacture shell and gun forgings. Large quantities of 4.7″ to 12″ shells were supplied for the British Government and equal quantities of 3″ and 4.7″ for the United States Government. Upon the entrance of the United States into the war the Government called upon the Company to supply 155 millimeter gun and 155 millimeter howitzer forgings.

The total area covered at the present time by buildings and yard is 119 acres. The main plant lies along the east bank of the Kishacoquillas Creek. Water pipes connected with a constant and abundant supply of water, are laid throughout the Works, with convenient outlets at various points.   A well-drilled fire department is maintained, manned and officered by the employees.

There are fifteen miles of track in and around the plant, owned by the Company, on which are operated nine steam locomotives, two electric locomotives, nine locomotive cranes, one self-propelled hoisting engine and eighty-one cars.

The entire plant is thoroughly modern in every particular with every labor-saving device incorporated.   It represents the progress of the iron and steel industry which has been continuous from the little forge of 1795, operated by water power and distributing its products by wagon, river and canal, to the extensively developed plant of 1920 with its diverse industries, capable of producing two hundred thousand tons of steel yearly and employing five thousand men.

INDEX

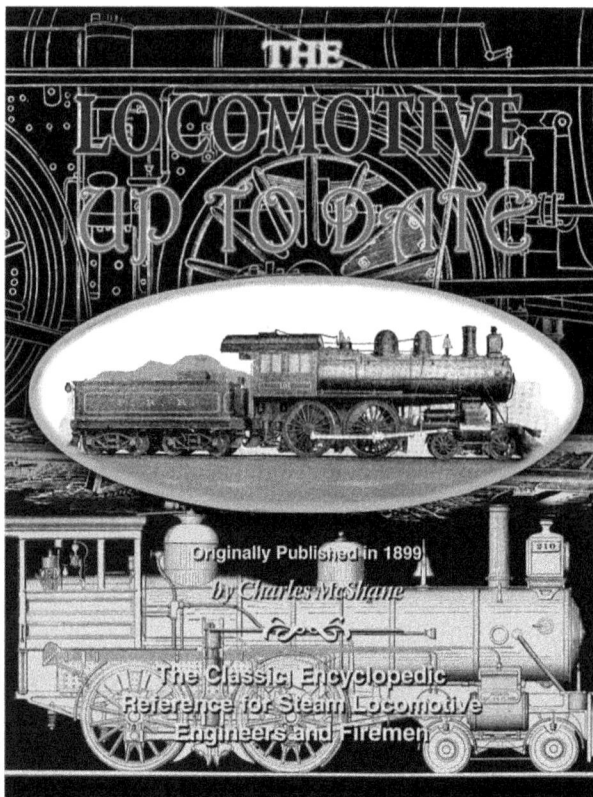
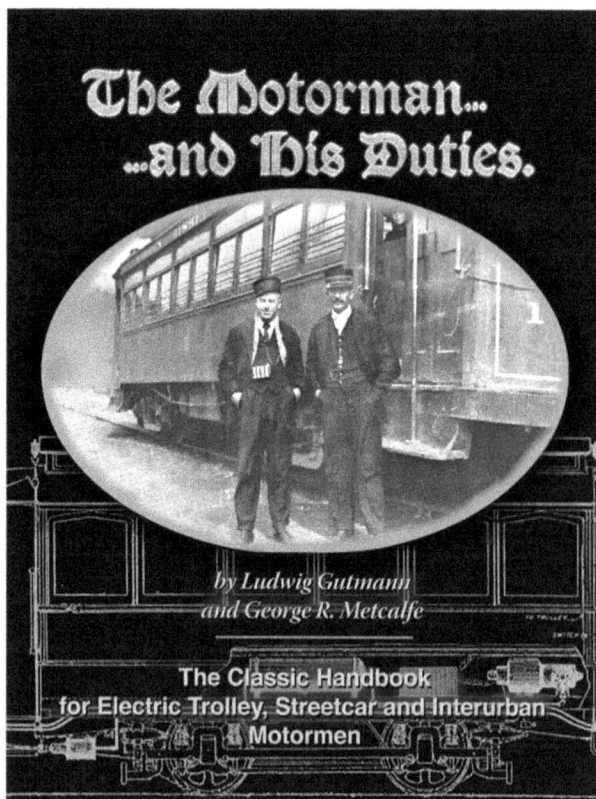

The New York Subway
ITS CONSTRUCTION AND EQUIPMENT

INTERBOROUGH
RAPID
TRANSIT
-1904-

Reprinted by PeriscopeFilm.com

On October 27, 1904, the Interborough Rapid Transit Company opened the first subway in New York City. Running between City Hall and 145th Street at Broadway, the line was greeted with enthusiasm and, in some circles, trepidation. Created under the supervision of Chief Engineer S.L.F. Deyo, the arrival of the IRT foreshadowed the end of the "elevated" transit era on the island of Manhattan. The subway proved such a success that the IRT Co. soon achieved a monopoly on New York public transit. In 1940 the IRT and its rival the BMT were taken over by the City of New York. Today, the IRT subway lines still exist, primarily in Manhattan where they are operated as the "A Division" of the subway. Reprinted here is a special book created by the IRT, recounting the design and construction of the fledgling subway system. Originally created in 1904, it presents the IRT story with a flourish, and with numerous fascinating illustrations and rare photographs.

Originally written in the late 1900's and then periodically revised, A History of the Baldwin Locomotive Works chronicles the origins and growth of one of America's greatest industrial-era corporations. Founded in the early 1830's by Philadelphia jeweler Matthais Baldwin, the company built a huge number of steam locomotives before ceasing production in 1949. These included the 4-4-0 American type, 2-8-2 Mikado and 2-8-0 Consolidation. Hit hard by the loss of the steam engine market, Baldwin soldiered on for a brief while, producing electric and diesel engines. General Electric's dominance of the market proved too much, and Baldwin finally closed its doors in 1956. By that time over 70,500 Baldwin locomotives had been produced. This high quality reprint of the official company history dates from 1920. The book has been slightly reformatted, but care has been taken to preserve the integrity of the text.

A HISTORY OF THE
BALDWIN
LOCOMOTIVE
WORKS
1831-1920

Reprinted by PeriscopeFilm.com

NOW AVAILABLE AT
www.PeriscopeFilm.com

www.ingramcontent.com/pod-product-compliance
Lightning Source LLC
Chambersburg PA
CBHW050352100426
42739CB00015BB/3367